Young People's Book of Law

Young People's Book of Law

L. L. BLAKE
*of the Middle Temple
and Gray's Inn, Barrister*

THE SHERWOOD PRESS

All rights reserved. No part of this publication may be reproduced or transmitted in any form or by any means including photocopying and recording, without the written permission of the copyright holder, application for which should be addressed to the Publishers. Such written permission must also be obtained before any part of this publication is stored in a retrieval system of any nature.

First published 1984

© L. L. Blake 1984

The Sherwood Press Ltd., 88 Tylney Road, London E7 OLY

ISBN 0 907671 14 4

Set in Baskerville by Book Ens, Saffron Walden, Essex
Printed and bound by Streetsprinters, Baldock, Herts.

Contents

1	What is Law?	1
2	Justice	11
3	Common Law	20
4	Statute Law	29
5	Judges and Courts	38
6	Lawyers	48
7	Torts	57
8	Contract	65
9	Property	73
10	Crime	81

Epilogue		91
Appendix A	A Common Law Judgment	93
Appendix B	Example of a Statute	117
Appendix C	The Writ of Summons	125
Appendix D	How to enter the legal profession	126
References		130
Index		134

Acknowledgements

The publishers are grateful to the following for permission to reproduce copyright material: to Butterworths for the common law judgment (Appendix A); to the Controller of Her Majesty's Stationery Office for the example of a statute (Appendix B: Crown Copyright); and to Butterworths and Oyez Publishing for the writ of summons (Appendix C).

Foreword

This book is about the principles of law, especially English Common Law, for young people entering their 'teens. It is hoped it will be useful both for those who will otherwise not be introduced to the subject, and as a supplement to 'O' and 'A' level studies where sometimes the texts are dry and tedious and young people are in danger of missing the point.

I have tried to make the material interesting, as well as informative, so that readers may have a grounding in their precious heritage of Common Law and freedom. We live, today, in a world which is increasingly becoming subject to tyranny, of one kind or another. It is a great pity if our young people grow up taking their liberty for granted, or even ignorant of its value and of the work of past centuries that has gone into its making.

Without such basic education in citizenship, children may well become prey to political jargon and notions which are so temporary and which may lead them later to accept changes that are fundamentally bad, simply through lack of knowledge.

I hope they find that reading or hearing about the law is fun!

Gray's Inn,
March, 1984

Especially for
the boys and girls of
St James and St Vedast Schools,
London

1
What is Law?

> ... of law there can be no less acknowledged, than that her seat is the bosom of God, her voice the harmony of the world, all things in heaven and earth do her homage, the very least as feeling her care, and the greatest as not exempted from her power ... all with uniform consent, admiring her as the mother of their peace and joy.—*Richard Hooker*

Everything we do or say comes under law of some kind or other. Most of the time we are not even aware of the law working: it is only when we do something which is not in accordance with law that we run into trouble. 'Outlaws' are men who think they can live outside the law, and they are always hiding and always in trouble! In films about the American Wild West, outlaws were men who could be gunned down because they had lost the protection of the law.

Just consider what might be a typical day in your life. You leave your house early in the morning, to go to school. When you return, late in the afternoon, you expect to find that it is still your house, and that another family has not moved in and taken over all your furniture. The law protects you. If another family did move in, without your parents' consent, then they would be guilty of 'trespass', which is an old word meaning, simply, 'passing across'. Having 'passed across' your boundary—the fence or the door which you call your own—without permission, they could be asked politely to leave, and if they still did not, force could be used to make them go. Even a policeman needs the warrant of a Court to come in and search your house.

On your way to school, no doubt you will walk or ride along the street. There are all sorts of laws governing behaviour in the street. Again, most of the time, we are not usually aware of them, because most of us behave naturally and peacefully, which is all that the law requires. In the old days the roads connecting towns and villages were called the 'King's Highway', because there the King's Peace ran, and he would protect you if you were abused or threatened while you went on your lawful journey. Still, today, the streets are lit at night not primarily so that people can see where to go, but to make it more difficult for thieves and robbers to operate. Such people do not like the light: they prefer to lurk in the darkness.

You certainly have the right to walk and ride along the highway, so long as you do not interfere with the equal right of others to do the same. You might even want to sit down and take a rest beside the highway. All this is called the right of 'free passage': but what it does not mean is standing still for a long period of time or causing a nuisance or an obstruction. Sometimes you will see a man with a barrow selling fruit beside the pavement. He keeps a good lookout for a policeman; and, when he sees a policeman coming, he simply pushes his barrow on down the street. They both know that he has not permission to stay there; but, as long as he keeps on the move, the policeman cannot do much about him.

A highway does not have to be a paved street: it can be something as simple as a path across fields. And, although you, as a member of the general public, have the right to walk along it, this does not mean necessarily that the public owns the soil over which the highway passes. Those who own the land on either side of the highway might still own the soil underneath it. In an old case heard in a Court of Law, a man went along a roadway waving his handkerchief and opening and shutting his umbrella—he did this in order to scare away birds which the Duke of Rutland and his friends were hoping to shoot. The Duke's men asked him to stop, but he would not do so, and they sat on him until the birds had passed over. It seems that the Duke owned all the land thereabouts, including the soil under the highway: therefore, the Judges said, the man was doing more than he was entitled to, on the highway. He was a trespasser, and the Duke's men could sit on him if he would not go peacefully on his way.

Let us suppose you take a bus to school. Then, when the bus arrives at the bus stop, it offers itself to you for transport to your destination. You accept the offer when you board the bus, and a contract, or binding agreement, is made. You must now pay the bus fare. If you do not do so, then you are in breach of contract, and the conductor can put you off. But, let us suppose you were unfortunate, and the conductor rang the bell and the bus started while you were halfway on and halfway off, so that you fell on the ground and hurt yourself: here, the law of tort would operate. 'Tort' is another old word, meaning 'twisted', that is, not straight, not right, but wrong. A tort is a wrongful act. Thus, if the conductor was careless as to whether you were on or off when he gave the signal to the driver to start, the bus company, for which the conductor worked, could be held liable to pay you money for the injury you have suffered. You might well ask, what is the use of money to me if I have lost a leg, for example? All the money in the world could not replace the use of that leg. Well, the law of tort says that all it can do, in money terms, is to put you back in the position you were in before the horrible accident occurred. If the injury was such that you could never work again, the bus company would have to give you so much money that it would keep you for the rest of your days.

And at school itself—hoping that you arrive safely, without losing a leg or being arrested for obstructing the highway—another set of laws applies. The Education Act of 1944 says that you must be educated, to proper standards, at school or elsewhere. That is why the teacher will tick your name in a register: if you fail to appear, and it happens regularly, then a school attendance officer will take you and your parents to Court in an effort to get you to obey. By law the school day begins with an act of 'collective worship', which means all the pupils gathering together to worship God. This, of course, recognises that education is not merely concerned with the development of mind and body, but with the soul, or spirit, of everyone as well.

All that we have just spoken about relates to 'doing', or your actions during the day. Now, what about 'saying'? How does the law govern what words you use, either in speaking them or writing them down? The law is very simple: you can speak or write any words you like, as long as they do not defame another person. What does 'defame' mean? It means to take away the fame, or good name, of someone else: you cannot go around saying that someone is a liar or cheat when he or she is not. Otherwise, if people you tell believe it, the person defamed may lose his or her job or their credit in the community.

This does not just apply to the words you say or write, but to pictures you draw or models you make. You must not portray someone in a way which, untruthfully, produces disharmony between him or her and the rest of the community. The law is all about harmony between people, as Richard Hooker says in the piece quoted at the start of this chapter. Once the famous Madame Tussauds, the waxworks museum in the centre of London, put an effigy in its Chamber of Horrors of a man who had actually not been found guilty of murder: as you can understand, to walk into the Chamber of Horrors and to find a waxwork of yourself on display there, in the company of men and women who had been hung for murder, was not a pretty sight for this man and did not do him any good in the eyes of his fellow-men. So the man was entitled to sue in a Court of Law for money damages for the insult to his reputation.

All of this appears to be perfectly natural. One does not even think of it, most of the time. We behave naturally and peaceably towards each other and the result is happiness; when we hurt or injure each other the result is bitterness between people and unhappiness.

Once there was a great judge, who lived in the eighteenth century. His name was Sir William Blackstone. He was a large, very fat man and it was said that he died through lack of exercise. But he wrote a most marvellous book of law, called *Commentaries on the Laws of England*, which really set the pattern of our thinking about the great Common Law of England for the past two centuries. In that book he wrote this:

> [the Creator] has not perplexed the law of nature with a multitude of abstract rules and precepts . . . but has graciously

reduced the rule of obedience to this one paternal precept, 'that man should pursue his own happiness'.

Now that statement has to be properly understood. What it does *not* mean is that we can all go out and do and get what we want without regard to any one else, acting selfishly and unreasonably, because the great test is, do our actions result in our own happiness? Obviously if what we do or say results in other people being hurt, shunning us, or even sending us to prison for our crimes, the result (for us) is not happiness but misery. Always the law works towards harmony between men: and the great hope is that when a man is sent to prison he will learn his lesson, by being shut off from the community for a time, so that in the end he will be restored to the harmony of his fellows.

You will note that Blackstone speaks of the law of nature as coming from God. He says that men are utterly dependent upon God and that if they obey God's simple law they will achieve happiness and freedom.

What is God's law that we have to obey? We find it stated in the Bible:

> Then one of them, which was a lawyer, asked him a question, tempting him, and saying,
>
> Master, which is the great commandment in the law?
>
> Jesus said unto him, Thou shalt love the Lord thy God with all thy heart, and with all thy soul, and with all thy mind.
>
> This is the first and great commandment. And the second is like unto it, Thou shalt love thy neighbour as thyself.
>
> On these two commandments hang all the law and the prophets.

One important thing to be noticed about that statement is that Jesus used the word 'shalt'—'Thou *shalt* love thy neighbour ...' There is no 'may' or 'might'; it is a commandment, and at the end of the day everyone will have to obey it. We live now in a predominantly Christian civilisation which was established for the good of Man two thousand years ago by Our Lord. So what Jesus says is the law for the civilisation we have inherited.

So much is it the law for our civilisation that the wise say that all the many man-made laws we live under today are just more complicated ways of saying the same thing, which was said, in fact, in those two simple commandments. A wise French lawyer of the seventeenth century, Jean Domat, wrote:

> However, although men have violated these fundamental laws (love thy God, love thy neighbour), and although society be in a state strangely different from that which ought to be raised upon these foundations, and cemented by this union; it is still true that these divine laws, which are essential to the nature of Man, remain immutable, and have never ceased to oblige men to the observance of them: and it is likewise certain ... that all the laws which govern society, even in the condition in which it is at present, are no other than consequences of these first laws.

To give a very simple example: when you drive a car along the highway you ought always to drive it and maintain your car in such a condition that it does not injure someone else, or damage their property. That is just plain common-sense. It is reasonable, because if everyone took the contrary view the road would be full of crashes. But it is just acting out the commandment to love your neighbour as yourself. As long as you act in this way, and other people act likewise, no-one will come to any harm.

But, as we all know, some people do not heed the simple commandment. They drive along the roads in such a way that they are a menace to everyone else. Then they must come under stronger laws which, if they disobey, can cause them to be fined or sent to prison. Such are laws and regulations which specify that cars must stop at red lights and at zebra crossings when pedestrians are using them; that car speeds are limited according to the kinds of road they are on; that older cars must be tested every year and that the rubber on tyres must be of a certain width and depth.

When you think about it, all these detailed laws and rules are doing the same thing, to *make* you love your neighbour as yourself. And that is what Jesus said, 'Thou *shalt* love thy neighbour as thyself'. The beauty of it is, that if you conduct yourself always on the roads so as not to injure someone else you are free of all the petty restrictions and will not have to face the traffic Court. For you know, naturally, that it is not safe for you or anyone else if you drive round on tyres that are old and bald of rubber.

So there are different levels, or kinds, of law in operation. First, there is divine law—the law of God, which is fundamental and may be discovered in the Bible and the other great scriptures of mankind. We rely on great men, such as Moses and Jesus, to tell us what the law of God is.

Second, there is natural law, so called because it is the law which arises from the nature of a person or thing. When someone designs something, like a clock, which is the example given by Blackstone, he puts into it certain laws which the clock must obey while it remains useful as a clock: thus the hands must move round the circle of the hour within that period of time, no more and no less. If the design of the clock is bad, then the result will be a clock that is no good to anyone, for it will just confuse and mislead whoever wishes to tell the time by it. We call it 'natural law' for a clock to tell the time correctly. What, then, is natural law for human beings? Sir William Blackstone says it is that law, implanted at the beginning of mankind, by the Creator, which requires people to seek their own real happiness. Man's true nature is to be happy, and that happiness is just a reflection of the Nature of the Creator himself.

Next we have the customs by which people live: long ago people were given by wise men ways of living and behaving which followed the law of God, and which the people found, through practice, brought them peace and harmony. If there was any question of what was right and proper, then they took their problems to a judge, a man who had long studied the scriptures and knew how to listen patiently and ask the right questions which would bring out the facts. This is of the utmost importance in any Court of Law: there is an old saying, 'the law arises from the facts'. It is no good trying to determine anything unless you have all the facts before you. Imagine someone coming along and saying, 'John killed Peter'. A judge would need to know how Peter was killed, with what weapon, who was there at the time, and what was John's state of mind, before he could begin to say whether it was murder or just an accident.

We call this third kind of law 'Common Law', because it is common to all the people. They live by it and pass it on down to their children, usually by example. Many judges over many centuries have laid down these safe paths for men and women to follow. The judges express and shape the law through the use of reason. One judge does not presume to know everything—he is guided by what other judges have said in the past. A judge today listens to everything that is said, reads what other great lawyers have said about similar situations, and, after reflection, declares what he thinks is the right answer to the problem he has to solve. If he gets it wrong (and judges can get it wrong—they are only human), there are courts of appeal where more senior judges can put things right.

What is this reason which judges use? Each one of us has the power of reason. We sometimes call it the 'light of reason'— and it is like this, a light in the mind which shows us clearly what is right and what is wrong, what is true and what is false. To get there, one has to keep asking questions. The mind sifts and sorts these questions until there are only one or two very basic questions left. Then the mind, in the face of these questions, falls very still; and the answer emerges, 'This is right, and that is wrong'.

It is always delightful to hear, or read about, reason at work. Socrates, the great philosopher, who lived in Athens about 2,500 years ago, loved reason and was always asking questions which led to reasonable conclusions. Here he is with his friends, Glaucon and Adeimantus, who want to know what justice is all about, and how it affects them.

> I told them, what I really thought, that the search would be no easy one, and would require very good eyes. Seeing then, I said, we are no great wits, I think we had better adopt a method which I may describe in this way; suppose a short-sighted person had been requested by some one to read small letters a long way off; and some one else told him that he had seen the

very same letters elsewhere written larger and on a larger scale—if they were the same and he could read the larger letters first, and then proceed to the lesser—that would have been thought a rare piece of good fortune.

Very true, said Adeimantus; but how does the illustration apply to us?

I will tell you, I replied; justice, which is the subject of our enquiry, is, as you know, sometimes spoken of as the virtue of an individual, and sometimes as the virtue of a state.

True, he replied.

And is not a state larger than an individual?

It is.

Then in the larger the quantity of justice will be larger and more easily discernible. I propose therefore that we enquire into the nature of justice and injustice as appearing in the state first, and secondly in the individual, proceeding from the greater to the lesser and comparing them.

Whenever something reasonable is said, the mind instantly agrees with it. The mind says, 'Of course. It's like that. It stands to reason'. What we appreciate is the statement which links all the parts together, and makes one, or unity, of them.

The fourth level of law is statute law, or law made by Parliament. When men cannot obey the simple requirements of reason, then stricter measures have to be brought into force, carrying penalties—imprisonment or fines—laid down by Parliament. Most lawyers now have long shelves of books containing all the statutes, or Acts of Parliament, which give very precise directions on how people shall behave. It just shows how careless men and women have become of each other, and how necessary it is that they be reminded, very precisely, of the simple commandment to love their neighbours as themselves. It was not so very long ago that cars had rear lights which were like small red buttons: now cars have huge red lights like slashes across the back of them, simply because drivers have become less observant of each other.

There is a fifth, and final, level of law which is harsh indeed. This is when people so far forget themselves, and their duties and responsibilities towards each other, that they allow a dictator to arise who will solve all their problems for them—usually at gunpoint, or with torture. A dictator is a man who claims to be above the law, and to know what is best for the state. He is supported by strong military and police forces. Then you cannot be free, but must become a slave. The horrifying thing is that a large part of the world now lives under tyranny of one kind or another. Our system of law, here in Britain, which keeps us free can only survive if we continue to behave responsibly. That means caring for and looking after other people—putting them first.

A writer called George Orwell once described what it would be like to live under total dictatorship, when even your thoughts came under control by the police. He tells how the hero of the book was in a street looking up at a huge sign on a tall, concrete building. The sign said: 'Ministry of Peace'. In fact it was the Ministry of War. Even words had become twisted, and people were made to hate, and not love, their neighbours.

Fortunately, tyranny cannot last. It sometimes seems to last for a long time, perhaps centuries, but then a new enlightenment, a new civilisation, comes along and lifts men's hearts and minds. Jesus was born in a time of great misery for mankind, two thousand years ago: but his example and teaching gave us the Christian civilisation which is still with us and is still powerful for good. Moreover, it is the basis of our law.

2
Justice

> The nearest we can get to defining justice is to say that it is what the right-minded members of the community—those who have the right spirit within them—believe to be fair.—
> *Lord Denning*

Lawyers are never liked very much. In one of Shakespeare's plays the mob are roused to go and 'kill all the lawyers'. In my room at Chambers, which is where barristers work when they are not in court, I have a cartoon showing a cow and two men obviously disputing ownership of the cow: one man is pulling her horns and the other man is pulling her tail. In between the two men, sitting on a low stool and milking the cow, sits a lawyer. This is meant to show that, while people dispute with each other over such things as ownership, the lawyers are the only people to gain.

When a famous Archbishop went to talk to a meeting of lawyers he started his address with these words: 'I cannot say that I know much about the law, having been far more interested in justice.' He was joking, of course; but there is more than a grain of truth in what he said. You cannot have law without a sense of justice.

So, what is justice?

There have been many attempts to define justice. The word itself comes from the distant past of language, from a Sanskrit word *yuj*, meaning to join, or to connect. We get another word from the same source, 'yoke', which usually gives rise to a mental picture of oxen carrying a wooden beam across their shoulders. But that word, too, means joining together. And when Jesus said

> Take my yoke upon you, and learn of me; for I am meek and lowly in heart; and ye shall find rest unto your souls.
> For my yoke is easy, and my burden is light,

He was inviting people to join Him in the work He had to do, which was nothing less than to redeem the whole of mankind.

You may remember that, in Chapter 1, we spoke of the famous philosopher, Socrates, telling the story of the shortsighted man who discovered that the words he wanted to read were elsewhere written large, and he was advised to read them first. Thus, says Plato, the man who recorded all that Socrates said, you may find justice written large in society before you look at what justice means for the individual person.

Plato speaks of justice again in these terms:

> 'Friends', we say to them,—'God, as the old tradition declares, holding in His hand the beginning, middle, and end of all that is, moves according to His nature in a straight line towards the accomplishment of His end. Justice always follows Him, and is the punisher of those who fall short of the divine law. To that law, he who would be happy holds fast, and follows it in all humility and order; but he who is lifted up with pride, or money, or honour, or beauty, who has a soul hot with folly, and youth, and insolence, and thinks that he has no need of a guide or ruler, but is able himself to be the guide of others, he, I say, is left deserted of God; and being thus deserted, he takes to him others who are like himself, and dances about, throwing all things into confusion, and many think that he is a great man, but in a short time he pays a penalty which justice cannot but approve, and is utterly destroyed, and his family and city with him.

Plato tell us, in this short passage from the book called *The Laws*, that law is a straight line. 'God,' he says, 'holding in His hand the beginning, middle and end of all that is'. Now, that straight line, or law of God, can be described in a different way, as cause, activity and result. You always have these three in the working of any law. Causes lie in nature; activity is in the mind; and the results we can always see around us in the physical world. By way of example, going back to Chapter 1, if the desire is to love your neighbour as yourself, you drive a car on the road with great care for everyone else who is using the same road, and the result is good order and the absence of accidents. On the other hand, if the desire is to drive as fast as possible, with no care for others, then the driving will be reckless and the results are likely to be fear and danger to other people and the occurrence of accidents. We call such results 'accidents', meaning that we do not intend them to happen, but in fact they are the working out of law.

Natural law, we are told by the wise, expresses the Will of God that all men should be happy. You will recall the words of the great lawyer, Blackstone, in Chapter 1, that the Creator requires every man to pursue his own real happiness. And that real happiness, in fact, lies nowhere else than in the nature of God Himself, which is full of knowledge, consciousness and bliss.

Accordingly, Plato says, the man who would be truly happy holds fast to God's law, 'and follows it in all humility and order'. Otherwise justice comes along and punishes those 'who fall short of the divine law'. His picture of the punishment of the man who has a soul 'hot with folly' is not a pretty one, resulting in the destruction of the man himself and his family and city. But here we have to bear in mind another word, 'mercy', which always goes with justice.

During the Coronation of our present Queen, she was asked by the Archbishop of Canterbury: 'Will you to your power cause Law and Justice, in Mercy, to be executed in all your judgments?' And the Queen promised: 'I will.' When she entered Westminster Abbey, in procession, one of the swords carried before the Queen had a flat, blunt end, rather than the sharp, pointed ends which you usually find on swords, and this weapon is called 'Curtana', or the Sword of Mercy. The name 'Curtana' comes from 'Courtain', the sword of Ogier the Dane, an eighth-century warrior. He was supposed to have drawn Courtain against an Emperor's son in revenge for the killing of his own son, but drew back when a voice from Heaven called upon him to show mercy.

This quality of mercy is something the Queen possesses and can use, when need be, to reward someone, which is its original meaning. We like to think of mercy as something which is given to someone to excuse them from their lawful punishment; but it is not that at all. The law works in a straight line, and cannot be changed. The penalty for not observing the law has to be paid, but it is possible, through knowledge, or conscience (which is a word to do with knowledge), that the damage suffered can be borne by someone stronger or by the people at large. Then mercy is extended to the individual wrongdoer. But this is only properly done when the man or woman concerned shows regret and signs that he or she will afterwards live an honourable life.

The Lord Chancellor, head of all the Queen's Judges, was at one time called the 'keeper of the King's Conscience'. In early times he was always a bishop or priest and, as such, he could advise the King about the state of men's souls and whether they meant it or not when they swore to behave themselves if they received mercy from the King. The word 'conscience' means 'with knowledge', and it really is knowledge of good and bad. The bishop or priest, acting as keeper of the King's Conscience, could say what effects a certain action would have, and whether it was possible for the King himself or his people to absorb the harmful effects of an action and give peace and mercy in return.

Gradually, as the King became busier with affairs of state, the Lord Chancellor himself sat in the Court of Chancery and gave judgments where people came to him, complaining of injustices suffered by them, for which they could not obtain relief in other courts. The Lord Chancellor became a lawyer rather than a bishop or priest. Whenever the law seemed unduly harsh, he would consider whether justice required him to be merciful towards the person who was in trouble.

This was called 'doing equity'. The word 'equity' means fairness, evenness, justice. In time, as various Lord Chancellors sat in the Court of Chancery, each one had different ideas of what was even, fair and just. A famous lawyer of the seventeenth century wrote that, in his view, equity changed according to the length of the Chancellor's foot. He was saying that, while the law itself was measured and precise, and you knew where you stood with the law, you could not depend on knowing what view the Lord Chancellor would take of your problems because it would change with each Chancellor, just as would the length of each Chancellor's foot. That did not seem very fair at all.

It is possible that all this arose from the loss of the religious influence in the Courts. When the Lord Chancellor was a churchman, he could tell the King what the divine law said, and what the state of men's souls required by way of mercy and justice. But when lawyers took on the important position of Chancellor they became, in time, less likely to have this kind of knowledge and to be more concerned with dry and dusty legal arguments.

In Charles Dickens' book, *Bleak House*, there is a very funny description of the Lord Chancellor in the nineteenth century sitting in Lincoln Inn's Hall, on a dark November afternoon with fog everywhere. He is supposed to be hearing a case which has dragged on for countless years. Everyone has forgotten almost how it began. And in the court there are miserable, faded people who have been trying to catch the Chancellor's eye for many long years. They try shouting out 'My Lord!', to catch his attention before he departs, for they want to get a decision from him on their many problems. But he is too quick for them, and scuttles out, before they can be heard. And they go away, sadly, to return another day in the hope that justice will be done. That state of affairs could not last: it was obviously unjust. One of the reasons Charles Dickens wrote that book was to show the misery that could result from the law's delays. Nowadays all courts are expected to apply equity as well as the law, so that it is not just left to one judge, the Lord Chancellor.

At the beginning of this chapter you will find what was said on the subject of justice by a very famous judge, Lord Denning. He was a judge for nearly forty years and sat in the highest courts in the land. He was greatly loved and respected for he gave everyone a patient hearing. His judgments are set out in clear, simple language, so that there can be no doubt about them; and they are full of reason and fairness towards his fellow-men. If you saw him in court, with his wig askew, his bright eyes darting about, and heard him speak in a broad, West Country voice, you would know you were in the presence of a great man, but one who was humble, too. Lord Denning is a devout Christian. It is often the mark of a truly great judge that he knows the scriptures and can draw on them to help him decide the cases which come before him.

Lord Denning says that the nearest we can get to defining justice is to say that it is what the right-minded members of the community—those who have the right spirit within them—believe to be fair. Now, these remarks echo what was said by the philosopher, Socrates, in Athens nearly 2,500 years ago. He said that injustice, the opposite of justice, meant being ruled by anger and fear, pleasure and pain, jealousies and desires. 'But when the opinion of the best . . . has dominion in the soul and orders the life of every man, even if it be sometimes mistaken, yet what is done in accordance therewith, and the principle in individuals which obeys this rule, and is best for the whole life of man, is to be called just.'

This may not be an easy passage to understand. But what it comes down to is this: the opinion of the best should guide our lives, and not the emotions of the moment, like anger and fear, pleasure and pain. Justice is being obedient to that rule, and not doing what we like, when we like. But who are the best and what is their opinion?

Socrates elsewhere describes it like this: suppose someone comes up to you in the street and asks you the way to a certain place. If you had actually been there, and knew how to get there, you would have knowledge and would quickly be able to tell that person the way. But perhaps you have never been there yourself: nevertheless you have heard someone with the necessary knowledge describe the way, and you would be able to pass it on. This would only be your opinion, based on what someone else told you, but it would be a good opinion, the 'opinion of the best', because it was based on knowledge of the journey.

So, says Socrates, it is with life. There are men who have

made the journey, men like Jesus, who know God, and therefore have knowledge which they communicate through the scriptures. Others listen very carefully to what the Masters say, and study; and, while they have not the full knowledge themselves, nevertheless they are obedient to the teachings and they are guides to all of us in our daily lives.

Even so, says Socrates, being human they can sometimes be wrong. Lord Denning was sometimes wrong in the judgments he gave (and admitted it): but that does not mean that we should constantly quibble and question what they tell us to do, because, in the main, what they tell us to do is for our own best interests.

Socrates himself was a case in point: he was condemned to die by a vote of the citizens of Athens, unjustly, when the minds of those citizens had been swayed by the 'anger and fear' provoked by a few, malignant men. He was offered the chance to escape by his friend Crito. But Socrates refused to escape. He said that he had been condemned to die by the laws of Athens, and he would not help to destroy the authority of those laws by leaving the country. After all, those same laws had given him birth and educated him and given him the opportunity to teach for so many years: how would it be if he set an example of disobeying them, when the same laws had led to his forthcoming execution? Socrates was a well-known, wise, and powerful figure. Future generations would not trust or follow the laws given them by such men as Socrates if he failed to obey them himself.

We get a sense of how men of true opinion draw on the scriptures for their guidance, and then lay down a path for the rest of us to walk in peace and harmony, in the work of another great judge, Lord Atkin. He had a great knowledge of the law and love of religious principles. Like all truly great judges, he was very concerned for the rights of the ordinary man and woman.

In 1932 he had to judge a very famous case concerning a girl who went into a cafe with a friend and drank ginger beer which was bought for her by her friend, and which was poured from a dark bottle. When she came to pour some more into her glass, out floated a dead snail which had been in the bottle. As a result of this, the poor girl became seriously ill because the drink had been poisoned by the decomposed body of the snail.

Several judges had wondered what to do about this case. They all probably wanted to help the girl and put a stop to this kind of thing happening again: but they did not, as the law stood at the time, know what to do. The café-owner was not to blame, because he had merely taken the dark bottle in good faith from the manufacturer, and could not have seen inside it before he took the metal cap off and started pouring the ginger beer. Was the manufacturer to blame? But he did not know the girl and it was not to her that the drink had been sold, but to her friend who was not injured by consuming it. Was a manufacturer to be liable to all and sundry, even to people who had not paid money for the goods he made? In any event, accidents can always happen in the best-run businesses, and the manufacturer had certainly not intended the snail to make its grave in one of his bottles!

When the case got to the House of Lords, the highest court in the land, Lord Atkin cut through all the indecision. He simply went back to the scriptures and said, you must love your neighbour as yourself. This meant, in law, you must not injure your neighbour. Who, then, is my neighbour? was the question put by Lord Atkin. He answered his own question by saying that one's neighbour is always someone you ought reasonably to have in mind when you are thinking about the acts you are about to do, such as filling bottles with ginger beer. It does not matter that the girl who drank it was many miles away—she was still the manufacturer's neighbour if he had thought about her best interests and had used every possible care to ensure that she would not be poisoned by his drink. Just as much care, in fact, as if she had actually lived next door to the manufacturer and been his neighbour in the usual sense of the word.

With this major decision of Lord Atkin a whole new field of law—the law of negligence—was really established for the first time. Now every manufacturer knows that he must take the utmost care with his products to see that they are not injurious in any way. But see how it was done: Lord Atkin simply took the commandment in the Bible and applied it to ordinary, everyday life.

Now everyone accepts that what Lord Atkin said was just. His was true opinion, the opinion of the best, based on the knowledge he had gained from the scriptures.

3
Common Law

> ... and this is the sacred and golden cord of reason, called by us the common law of the State.—*Plato*

If we had lived in the fifteenth century, say, we might one day have seen a small troop of men riding on horses across the countryside towards a market town. In their midst rode a man in scarlet robes wearing on his head a close-fitting white silk cap with a black skull-cap on top of it: and, today, if you look at a judge's wig you will see a small circle on top, representing the white cap, or 'coif' as it was called, which the judges used to wear. For this man on horseback was one of the King's Judges, an 'itinerant' or travelling justice, one of a number sent out by the King across the length and breadth of the land to decide cases in the King's name.

This idea of sending out royal judges came from one of our greatest and wisest Kings, Henry II, who reigned from 1154 to 1189. He was concerned that ordinary people should have justice in their local courts, but that they might not get it from powerful and arrogant noblemen. We still have the records of King Henry's decision to send out judges:

> The bishops, earls and magnates of the realm being assembled at Windsor [in the year 1179], the king by their common counsel ... divided England into four parts. For each part he appointed wise men from his kingdom and later sent them through the regions of the kingdom assigned to them to execute justice among the people ... Thus he took care to provide for men's needs by setting apart from the generality of mankind those who, albeit they live among men and watch over them, yet possess qualities of insight and boldness superior to those of an ordinary man.

Still, today, nearly 900 years later, the royal judges go out on circuit through the country, determining those matters which require great skill and long experience in the law. Only, these days, they do not ride on horseback, but by train or by car. It is still an important event when one of Her Majesty's Justices attends court in a country town, bringing out trumpets and uniforms and policemen saluting.

Why was it such an important step, this sending out 'wise men' to do justice in the King's name?

It marked the beginning of the Common Law of England which is the foundation of our freedom and the great gift we have made to English-speaking countries throughout the world. What it meant was this: the wise men, the judges, would inquire into the customs by which men lived in their localities; they would discuss them amongst themselves when they returned to Westminster; and they would allow those customs to continue which were reasonable and good for the people. In time, therefore, the judges built up a system of common customs, or law common to the whole of England: but it was law acceptable to the people because it represented what they had lived by for generations and because it accorded with reason. The law was not imposed by the king, by strength of arms; but it was given with the consent of the people.

In an earlier age, the founder of the English nation, the one King whom we call 'Great', King Alfred, did much the same thing when he published his Laws. He tells us, in the introduction to those laws:

> 'Then I, King Alfred, collected these together and ordered to be written many of them which our forefathers observed, those which I liked; and many of those which I did not like, I rejected with the advice of my councillors, and ordered them to be differently observed. For I dared not presume to set in writing at all many of my own, because it was unknown to me what would please those who should come after us. But those which I found anywhere, which seemed to me most just ... I collected herein, and omitted the others. Then I, Alfred, King of the West Saxons, showed these to all my councillors, and then they said that they were all pleased to observe them.'

Notice the humility of this great King. He does not claim credit for the laws, but says he chose those which were most just and showed them to his councillors who approved them for the people. These were not new laws, but laws 'which our forefathers observed'—or, at least, those which were reasonable and just and which were appropriate to the times in which Alfred lived.

In one of the oldest scriptures known to mankind, the Laws of Manu, it is stated:

> A king who knows the revealed law must inquire into the particular laws of classes, the laws or usages of districts, the customs of traders, and the rules of certain families, and establish their peculiar laws, if they be not repugnant to the law of God;
> Since all men, who mind their own customary ways of proceeding, and are fixed in the discharge of their several duties, become united in affection with the people at large, even though they dwell far asunder.

This is not at all an easy passage to understand. Put simply, it says that the king is taken to know the divine law, the law of God: and if he does not know it, he will have priests and wise men to tell him what the law of God is. That law is the 'golden met-wand', or measuring stick, by which all other laws are judged. The king should let all the different classes of people—traders, soldiers, town councillors, old-established families, and so forth—have their own laws to conduct their affairs, because they are accustomed to these laws which bring them together and make them affectionate towards each other. 'Accustomed', you will see, is another word to do with 'custom', which comes from the Latin language and means 'one's very own'. However, should those local customs run contrary to the law of God—if they should be unjust or unreasonable—then, under the very old Hindu scriptures of Manu, the king would have to interfere and change them.

We still have word-pictures of those old judges going about the country in medieval times, inquiring into local customs and judging whether they were reasonable; and, in the process, building up the Common Law of England. Here is one such word-picture taken from a Year Book of 1469. These Year Books are early reports of what was said and done in the Courts, and they may have been written by students of law who had to listen to the judges in order to get their training in the law.

This case took place in Kent. A man who owned some land beside the sea complained that fishermen would come up from the sea and dig holes in his land into which they would drive stakes and hang on them their fishing nets to dry. He was more than a little peeved at this behaviour, going down to his land and finding the place full of nets. He sued in trespass, which, as you may remember from Chapter 1, is an old word meaning passing across my land without permission, and he asked the royal judges to stop it happening. The defence was that 'all the men of Kent' had been used from time immemorial, when fishing in the sea, to dig in adjoining land in order to pitch stakes to hang out and dry their nets. Here is what the judges said. Each judge's name has a 'J' after it, and this means 'Justice'. So Choke J. means 'Mr Justice Choke' and you know from this that he was one of His Majesty's Justices of the King's Bench. Also, when the judges speak, you will have to bear in mind that they are addressing their remarks to the barristers, or lawyers, appearing for the opposite sides:

> *Choke J.*:'This custom cannot be good, for it is against common right to prescribe to dig in my land, but there are other customs, which are used throughout the whole land, and such customs are legal: for example, that of innkeepers who are chargeable for the goods of their guests, if the goods are stolen. And also there is another custom that if my neighbour guard his fire negligently, so that through his negligence my house is burned, he will be liable to me: and such customs are good.'
>
> *Littleton J.*: 'Custom which prevails throughout the whole land is common law ... And, Sir, a custom which can stand upon reason shall be allowed, for example the custom [which allows the eldest son to inherit]; but this custom is against reason, for if he can dig in one place, he can dig in another. And so if a

man had a meadow adjoining the sea, they [the fishermen] by this custom could destroy the whole meadow which would not be reasonable.'

As you can gather, the royal judges were not in favour of a custom which meant digging up someone else's land, and so they would not let it continue.

So the medieval judges of the King's Bench, in collecting together these local customs, and looking at them, and deciding which were reasonable and good for the people, were laying down paths of conduct that people could safely follow for generations. And also, of course, they established new customary ways of proceeding, through their decisions. Behind all customs, that people follow naturally and willingly, there are wise men who lay down the direction in which true happiness lies: that is, in how to love my neighbour as myself. Judges, therefore, through the use of reason in their judgments, declare the law as it always is, unchanging, permanent and wise.

Nowhere is this clearer than in the custom which the judges early on set for themselves, in England, that they would always give reasons for their decisions. There is no Act of Parliament, or rule made by the King, requiring judges to state reasons in giving their judgments. But they always do; and if, today, a judge were to refuse to give his reasons, then a dissatisfied party could go to a higher court and obtain an order for him to do so. This is tremendously important. When a judge has heard all the evidence, and the speeches made by the barristers for both sides, then he gives his judgment orally—that is, by word of mouth. And in stating out loud what the law is one can actually hear whether or not what is being said is reasonable. The practice has grown up of writing out judgments, which means giving them to the parties perhaps months after the trial has taken place—but this is not so satisfactory as hearing the judge state the law, out loud, even if he delays giving judgment while he reflects on it.

Then, if the judge appears to have gone wrong in his reasoning, the matter can be taken to the Court of Appeal, or perhaps even to the House of Lords, the highest court in the land, where other and more senior judges can put matters right. Can you imagine living in a country where judges are not required to give reasons for what they propose to do? There are such countries and freedom in them is not very great. The essential ruling principle in British government is that 'the king must not be under man but under God and the law, because law makes the king'. This means that the Queen and all her servants, including the judges, are under the same law, and must obey it, and must give their reasons for acting in the way they do.

At the back of this book, in Appendix A, you will find set out an interesting judgment given by a famous judge in the case of *Behrens* v. *Bertram Mills Circus*, decided in 1957. This was a sad and yet also funny little case, involving two midget people, husband and wife, who worked in a circus. One day, as the circus elephants were passing the tent in which the midgets lived, a dog sprang out and barked at the elephants who got frightened. One of the elephants called Bullu went after the little dog and trampled on the tent wherein was the midget wife. As a result, she was seriously injured, and her husband could not get work for some time because he was lost without her. Fortunately, they both recovered; and the judge had to decide whether the circus were liable in money damages to the midget husband and wife for the injuries and loss suffered.

When you read this judgment you will notice how carefully and thoroughly all the facts are stated. It is no good trying to decide anything, without knowing all the facts. It is a maxim of the law that the law arises from the facts. When all the facts have been sifted and arranged in their order of importance, then the mind can come to rest and, in the light of reason, the questions which have arisen, based on the facts, become simplified. Finally, there are perhaps one or two questions left which the judge has to answer. If the mind is quiet and still, often enough the answer emerges: such-and-such is right and such-and-such is wrong. Reason acts like this, connecting all the many parts with the whole: so that in a judgment everything falls into place around the knowledge of what is right, and the reasons the judge has to state in words flow from that right knowledge. You can see the results in what is called the 'headnote' of the judgment where, after the facts, the barrister reporting the case has collected together the reasons given by the judge for his decision.

You will see, when you read this case, how thoroughly the judge considered other judgments in previous cases. These are meant to assist him in coming to his conclusions. All judges respect what other judges have said on the same subject in the past. It is a continuing process, with each judge adding his contribution. A very great lawyer of the seventeenth century, Chief Justice Coke, wrote:

> ... if all the reason that is dispersed into so many several heads were united into one, yet could he not make such a law as the law in England is; because by many successions of ages it hath been fined and refined by an infinite number of grave and learned men, and by long experience grown to such a perfection, for the government of this realm, as the old rule may be justly verified of it ... No man out of his own private reason ought to be wiser than the law, which is the perfection of reason.

So all these wise men emphasise how important reason is to the Common Law. Indeed, that same Chief Justice Coke once said: '... for reason is the life of the law, nay the common law itself is nothing else but reason ...' And it all began a very long time ago because, as you can see from the quotation at the beginning of this chapter, Plato himself writing over 2,000 years ago says in *The Laws* that the golden cord of reason is the common law of the State.

How does this great system of law, the Common Law of England and of the other English-speaking countries in the world (including the United States of America), compare with other systems of law?

Really, there is one other important system of law in the world today, which is based on Roman Law. The Romans, when they conquered all the known world, some 2,000 years ago, gave very precise laws to the dominions over which they ruled. Today, Roman Law is the basis of law for all the countries of the continent of Europe—countries such as France, Germany, Belgium and Holland. Roman Law springs from an idea which was expressed in Latin thus: *Quod principi placuit legis habet vigorem, cum populus ei et in eum omne suum imperium et potestatem conferat.* This says, in effect, that law is what the prince (or king) says it is, for the people have given him their authority and power.

Now, that can be a dangerous idea in the wrong hands, because it can lead to the ruler saying what the law shall be without considering the wishes of the people. From quite early on, the independent English would have nothing to do with this idea. Their views were expressed by Chief Justice Fortescue in the fifteenth century:

> For the king of England is not able to change the laws of the kingdom at pleasure, for he rules his people with a government not only regal but also political. If he were to preside over them with a power entirely regal, he would be able to change the laws of his realm, and also impose on them taxes and other burdens without consulting them; this is the sort of dominion which Roman Laws indicate when they state that what pleased the prince has the force of law. But the case is far otherwise with the king ruling his people politically, because he is not able himself to change the laws without the assent of his subjects nor to burden an unwilling people with strange taxes, so that, ruled by laws that they themselves desire, they freely enjoy their properties, and are despoiled neither by their own king nor any other.

The English would not be told by others what to do; but wanted to be ruled by their own laws to which they gave assent. It is a priceless gift, this freedom which the English-speaking peoples cherish: but it can only work if everyone observes *duties* towards each other. Those duties really come down to this: not to hurt anyone else or their property. In other words, the English freedom is based on loving your neighbour as yourself. And the word 'freedom' comes to us from our Anglo-Saxon past—the word 'free' means 'dear' or 'friend', and 'dom' means 'doom', which is our old word for law or place. So it is the law of friends.

However, recently this country has become a member-state of the European Economic Community, which means that, to some extent, we have to accept Roman Law principles at work in our daily life. For the Commissioners of the EEC are very powerful men and, indeed, what pleases them has the force of law. It is too early to tell whether the independent nature of the English will accept all the rules which come from Europe: but already we have had to accept changes in our way of life, including what kind of milk we shall drink and the kind of punishment that can be inflicted in schools.

Roman Law depends on someone in authority writing down all the things we can do. The state gives permission for certain kinds of activity. For example, in Europe they have Bills of Rights which tell you what 'right' you can have, to do certain things, provided you behave yourself properly. This is all very different from the English Common Law, where everyone can do just as he or she pleases, so long as they do not hurt anyone else.

Lord Denning said, about EEC law, 'As so often happens with high-sounding principles, they have to be brought down to earth. They have to be applied in a work-a-day world'. This is true. The English Common Law is most practical. For it depends on the *facts* of everyone's situation, and not on what the rulers think might or could be best for all their subjects.

4
Statute Law

> Parliament can do everything but make a woman a man, and a man a woman. —*De Lolme*

The tiny Sanscrit word *stha*, meaning 'to stand', gives rise to a whole host of words in the English language, such as 'state', 'statute', 'constitution' and so forth. All these words have to do with men and women and where and how they stand, and what gives them the power to act in the way they do. The 'state' gives a man power to act as a judge: it gives him standing, or 'status'. If the state takes the power away, the man can no longer act as a judge. An 'estate' is a person's property which enables him or her to live in a certain way, and to afford, say a Rolls-Royce car. We call such a car a 'status symbol', which means that the owner is considered to be really quite wealthy, and therefore able to do things which cost a lot of money.

So when we come to consider statute law we are dealing with law made in writing by Parliament, which seeks to give status, or standing, to certain ideas or certain people for a period of time. It is temporary law. In the Common Law which we discussed in the last chapter, judges are always seeking to express, through the use of reason, the permanent, unchanging law: the law that always is. But Parliament is, or should be, only concerned with temporary grievances, the troubles of the moment, which, when righted, send people happily on their way.

This is quite clearly seen when you look at all the long line of books in any Law Library which contain all the statutes made by Parliament virtually since it came into existence in its present form, in about 1295. Many of the old statutes have long since fallen into disuse, their time having gone; and, every so often, lawyers have to go through them and weed out the old ones which no longer apply. And it is a principle that, if Parliament later passes an Act, or statute, which is at odds with an earlier statute, the earlier one no longer prevails.

Four hundred years ago some great judges of the time, called Barons of the Exchequer, met to consider what were the rules judges should observe when putting into effect an Act of Parliament, which is another name for a statute. The four rules which they set down are still, today, followed by the judges in courts of law. They are:

... (1st). What was the common law before the making of the Act. (2nd). What was the mischief and defect for which the common law did not provide. (3rd). What remedy the Parliament hath resolved and appointed to cure the disease of the commonwealth. And, (4th). The true reason of the remedy ...

Then, said the Barons of the Exchequer, having considered all these points, judges would do all in their power to effect the will of Parliament with regard to the cases which came before them for hearing.

This sets it all out quite simply. The natural state of affairs is that people live quite happily under the Common Law, their own law, the law of duties. But if something drastic happens, and the people fall sick, or neglect their duties, then Parliament has to step in, like a doctor, and prescribe medicine. The medicine might be rather nasty: never mind, if it effects a cure, the patient will go away strong again. So the people, if an Act of Parliament cures 'the disease of the commonwealth', can return to their accustomed ways of life under the Common Law.

The natural state of affairs is, therefore, the Common Law of England and Wales. It is the permanent background to people's lives. The Common Law fills all the spaces between statutes. If all the statute books got burned, and people could not remember what was said in them, we would still have the Common Law to live by: provided always that we remained healthy, which means observing and keeping the duty to love our neighbours as ourselves.

Acts of Parliament are always well intentioned. Parliament always tries to do its best for the people. But often statutes are clumsy attempts at medical first-aid, for they try in general words to cover all possible situations which might arise, and they lead to some odd results. Judges are bound to go by the words which Parliament has set down, but often you will hear senior judges say, in exasperation, that they cannot understand the words Parliament has used, or that they would like to do justice in a particular case, but the statute prevents them. Or, quite simply, they fall back on the Common Law and use reason to guide them.

There is quite a good little illustration in the Factories Acts. In the nineteenth century Parliament became concerned—with very good reason—at the working conditions in the factories which were springing up all over the country, to provide all the many goods which people were demanding. Men, women and children had been forced away from their villages and the land which had given them sustenance, to the towns and cities where the air was black with the smoke of the factories. Here even small children were set to work for long hours in hideous conditions to make profits for the factory-owners. There was appalling misery and poverty. No-one could say that the duty to love one another was being observed. And even the Common Law judges seemed powerless to intervene, saying bleakly that it was all to do with contracts of employment which people were free to enter or not to enter as they chose. This was small consolation to starving families who had been driven from the countryside by ruthless landowners! Parliament had to do something to 'cure the disease of the commonwealth'.

It did so by passing a number of Factories Acts. These, in the first place, were designed to reduce the number of hours small children and women had to work in the soot-laden buildings. Then, later, Parliament got round to specifying conditions of health, safety and welfare which people could expect while they were doing their jobs. In particular, of course, Parliament wanted to protect working men and women from dangerous machinery which unscrupulous employers might expect them to use without safeguards. And so we come to part of the current Factories Act, dated 1961, in which it is said as follows:

> Section 29 (2): Where any person has to work at a place from which he will be liable to fall a distance more than six feet six inches, then, unless the place is one which affords secure foothold and, where necessary, secure hand-hold, means shall be provided so far as is reasonably practicable, by fencing or otherwise, for ensuring his safety.

This seems quite straightforward: if someone has to work in a high place, more than six feet six inches above the floor, then the Act says his employer must provide him with hand-holds or footholds so that he does not fall off. You would think that, in any case, a good employer with the interests of his workers at heart would naturally see to it that the man was safe. But supposing that the man is working at a height of six feet five and a half inches above the floor, and he slips and falls and the employer has not provided a safe place to work. What then? Is the employer still liable to his workman for the injury he suffers? Under the statute he is not, because protection only starts when the workman is at least six feet six inches above the ground: a difference of one half inch! The workman would have to depend on the Common Law of Negligence for any redress he might have against his employer. Thus the Common Law fills in all the gaps in statutes and is much more important, in the long run, than Acts of Parliament.

Do you see how rigid and inflexible a statute can be? It is well meant; but general words cannot possibly cover all the situations that men find themselves in. Whereas the Common Law looks at all the facts that arise in a particular situation and determines from those facts, through reason, what the law is for that particular case. As stated in the last chapter, the Roman Law practised in France and other countries on the Continent of Europe is based on general statements of law built up into codes, or series of statutes: and if you happen to be unlucky enough to find yourself in a situation which is not covered by the codes then the law does not protect you.

Statute Law 33

But the shelves of the Law Libraries are now packed with great, fat volumes of Acts of Parliament. If you looked through them you would think there was no longer any space for the Common Law. Judges must spend most of their time trying to understand, and apply, long and complicated statutes. Parliament has been very busy, especially over the last forty years or so, passing more bills into Acts of Parliament. Indeed, they have grown so used to it that they think they are not doing anything useful unless they pass hundreds of bills into law: yet, at one time, statutes were rare and Parliament, the 'great debate of the nation', really had time to consider the problems the people might have to face in the future.

In a way, as we have seen in Chapter 1 of this book, it is a natural development of the law if people do not individually carry out their duties to one another. The Common Law is built on duties; and, if people fail to observe them, then Parliament has to step in and lay down quite precisely what men and women have to do so that the simple commandment to love your neighbour as yourself is fulfilled. One of the most frightening things about the Acts of Parliament which have been passed in recent years is the number of them which contain penalties of periods of imprisonment for failure to obey them. So the increasing number of statutes is a danger signal and a warning that we are beginning to hand over our precious freedom to government officials. One needs to remember that the Common Law says that everyone is free to do what he or she wants, provided always that it does not hurt anyone else: whereas a statute tells you what you can or cannot do, and sets out the limits of your freedom.

It is very important, in this country, that everyone is free and willing to carry out his or her duties. Because here is the home of liberty. The English set an example to the rest of the world and have given to other peoples the rich gifts of Parliamentary rule and the Common Law. Everywhere our Queen goes, in her travels across the world, she is loved, admired and respected. When one of our greatest judges, Lord Denning, spoke to gatherings in foreign countries he was listened to by thousands of people. The Speaker of the House of Commons is always considered to be the leading authority on Parliamentary democracy.

Two hundred years ago, in the House of Commons, the statesman Edmund Burke spoke about this, telling the Members of Parliament of their responsibility to other countries to maintain the principles of freedom. He ended by saying, 'Freedom they can have from none but you'.

Sir William Blackstone, the eighteenth-century judge and writer of the *Commentaries on the Laws of England*, said that this freedom consisted in men pursuing their own real happiness. He did not attempt to say what things would make men happy, but he did say that their happiness had to be real. It would be no good pretending that if you went out and did something which made others miserable and bitter towards you this would lead to real happiness as far as you were concerned.

There was a young student, called Jeremy Bentham, who sat listening to Blackstone when he gave his lectures on law at the University of Oxford. Bentham could hardly sit still, he was so angry at what he heard. He wanted to change things and he thought that people like Blackstone were so pleased with themselves and the state of English law as they found it that they would do nothing about some of the monstrous injustices of the time. Lots of students feel like this when they go to university; and being young, and impatient, they want to make the world a better place, according to their own ideas of how that should be. Later they realise that such changes come about by moderate and sensible reform and not by overthrowing all the good things that have been done in the past.

Anyway, Jeremy Bentham set about attacking Blackstone in books which he wrote after he left university. One of the most powerful sentences he ever wrote was this: 'The greatest happiness of the greatest number is the foundation of morals and legislation.' It was powerful because it was the idea behind all modern governments trying to do things for the good of most of the people through many, many Acts of Parliament. 'Legislation' means 'making laws', and this is what Parliament has tried to do, increasingly since Bentham's time, in order to make people happy.

What Bentham wrote was not at all the same as what Blackstone said. Blackstone did not confine his remarks to the 'greatest number'—he said that *all* men should be happy, and not just the greatest number, which would mean that some people would have to go on being miserable. Also, Blackstone did not think that a government official somewhere was able to dictate what should or should not make people happy, and lay down precise rules in Acts of Parliament as to how this should be achieved. But this is what has been happening ever since. Many governments since Bentham's day, acting on his ideas, have thought they knew best how to make most of the people happy. Perhaps it is changing now: because, in the end, English people especially do not like being told what they can and cannot do, and know that their traditional freedom is likely to be the best path to happiness.

But Parliament is still supreme. It is the Queen, the House of Lords and the House of Commons which, together, act for the good of the country: that is why a statute is called an 'Act' of Parliament. The judges must obey and enforce what Parliament has declared to be the law for the time being. At the beginning of this chapter you will find an amusing little quotation from a Swiss lawyer of the eighteenth century, De Lolme, who said that the English Parliament had the power to do anything except to make a man into a woman and a woman into a man. What he meant was that, as far as government is concerned, there is no higher authority in the country.

It used to be called 'The High Court of Parliament' and this was how it was seen in its earliest days, when there was no separation between what the courts did and the government of the realm. Indeed, even today, the highest court in the land is to be found in the House of Lords. Here sit the 'Law Lords', very senior judges who are also members of the House of Lords, led by the Lord Chancellor. You might be disappointed to see them at work, because they none of them wear rich red gowns and long wigs: just elderly gentlemen in dark suits sitting round a long table.

The idea was, in earliest times, that the people would bring their great grievances to the attention of Parliament: grievances which were too big for the local courts. They would present petitions, signed by lots of people, to the High Court of Parliament, and if Parliament agreed that there was merit in their cause the matter would be put into a 'Bill' requesting the King to redress the grievance. Still, today, when the House of Commons or the Lords are discussing a measure it is called a 'Bill' right up to the time when the Queen gives her assent, when it becomes an 'Act' of Parliament. Then, later, when it became necessary for the King to raise money for the many tasks of government, such as paying his troops and officers of state, Parliament insisted that the King listen to the grievances contained in the Bills, and do something about them which would help the people, before they would vote him money to come from taxes which the people would have to pay. This is still the principle, and only the House of Commons is allowed to levy taxes, in exchange for the Queen's Ministers agreeing to put matters right.

Chief Justice Coke, in the seventeenth century, once said that 'when an Act of Parliament is against common right and reason, or repugnant, or impossible to be performed, the Common Law will control it and adjudge such Act to be void'. It is very doubtful whether modern judges would be bold enough to say that, even though they may be tempted at times to think (or say) that an Act of Parliament is plainly nonsense. There are countries, such as the United States of America, which have written constitutions where the Supreme Courts are given the power to control Acts of the legislature: but here we like to think of judges and Parliament and ministers all working together for the common good, and not attacking each other. So judges will always try to effect the plain will of Parliament and, where there is doubt or confusion in the words used in an Act, the judges will give it the meaning best suited to the purpose of Parliament as they understand it to have been. But, unless the statute is very clear indeed, they will not give it a meaning which will intrude on the privacy and liberty of the people.

In Appendix B of this book you will find set out a short Act of Parliament with all the parts described. If you want to find out more about Parliament, and how it governs, perhaps you could read another book I have written, called *Young People's Book of the Constitution.*

5
Judges and Courts

> I do swear by Almighty God that I will do right to all manner of people after the laws and usages of this Realm without fear or favour, affection or ill-will.—*Oath sworn by judges on appointment*

In Anglo-Saxon times, just over a thousand years ago, the judges who would sit in a court of law were the bishop, the earldorman (we now call him an earl) and the sheriff. We think of a sheriff as a man with a badge who totes a gun and goes out looking for outlaws in Western films: and, in a way, this is right, for the early American settlers copied the name from the English 'shire-reeve', or shire officer, the man responsible for executing the law in a county.

An Anglo-Saxon king, Edgar, said: 'Let there be present the bishop of the shire and the earldorman and there both expound as well the law of God as the secular law.' This was important, for the King recognised that God's law and man's law run together, and are the same. It was necessary to have the bishop present, because he could tell the others what, according to his study and opinion, the law of God was in respect of a particular case. This link has never entirely been lost in English law, and gives it its strength. 'Christianity,' said one great judge, 'is parcel of the laws of England,' meaning that English law depends on Christian teaching. We have seen how true that is in a previous chapter, when we spoke of the snail-in-the-ginger-beer-bottle case, when the judge went straight to the scriptures for guidance.

You may have seen that excellent film, *A Man for All Seasons*, which was the story of Sir Thomas More, Lord Chancellor under King Henry VIII, a brave lawyer who stood up to the king when Henry thought he was bigger than the law. There is a part of the play when More, his wife Alice and his future son-in-law, William Roper, are together. They have just been visited by an oily character, called Richard Rich, who will later betray More to the king. Alice and the hot-headed young man, Roper, both think that Sir Thomas More should have arrested Rich before he caused mischief. Here is what they say:

Alice: While you talk, he's gone!
More: And go he should if he was the devil himself until he broke the law!
Roper: So now you'd give the Devil benefit of law!
More: Yes. What would you do? Cut a great road through the law to get after the Devil?
Roper: I'd cut down every law in England to do that!
More: Oh? And when the last law was down, and the Devil turned round on you—where would you hide, Roper, the laws all being flat? ... This country's planted thick with laws from coast to coast—Man's laws, not God's—and if you cut them down—and you're just the man to do it—d'you really think you could stand upright in the winds that would blow then? Yes, I'd give the Devil benefit of law, for my own safety's sake.

Sir Thomas More speaks there of England being planted thick with laws, and man's laws at that. But he also talks of the devil who will do evil if all the laws are cut down. This just reflects the fact that evil will succeed if we do not follow the laws which wise men have laid down for our protection. So it was important, in this case, not to arrest Richard Rich until he had acted unlawfully. This illustrates the great fairness of English law: but it also tells us that law protects us from evil, from the devil, who is the opposite of God.

When Duke William of Normandy conquered this country in 1066, he removed the bishops from the local courts. The bishops, he said, were not to judge in matters concerning the people but only in church affairs. King William, and the Norman kings who followed him, wanted to be the strong, central authority in all matters, including justice; and, no doubt, the influence of the bishops might not have allowed that to happen. Instead, as we have seen, by the time his great-grandson, Henry II, came to the throne, highly intelligent servants of the King were being sent across the country to establish a Common Law built on reason. Local customs were upheld only if they accorded with reason. It was a time when, to use the beautiful words of one writer, local custom 'curtsied to great kings'.

But judges continued to be devout men. They recognised that, in order to judge properly, they had to know the scriptures. Here is a description of a judge's day, written by Sir John Fortescue in about 1470:

> I also wish you to know that the justices of England do not sit in the king's courts except for three hours a day, that is, from eight o'clock before noon to eleven o'clock, because those courts are not held in the afternoon.... Hence the justices, after they have refreshed themselves, pass the whole of the rest of the day in studying the laws, reading Holy Scripture, and otherwise in contemplation at their pleasure, so that their life seems more contemplative than active. They thus lead a quiet life, free of all worry and worldly cares. Nor was it found that any of them was corrupted with gifts or bribes.

Not many busy modern judges would recognise themselves in those words! They are lucky if they can get out of court by four in the afternoon. But the points made by Sir John Fortescue are still very important ones: that judges need to know the sources of law; that they need to have quiet minds when they approach the clamour of the courts; and they should be so maintained by the state that they do not have to worry about money matters. It would never do for judges to be bribed by gifts of money to give judgments in a certain way. Our judges are quite independent; they cannot be removed from office unless they behave very badly indeed; and no-one in government can tamper with their salaries if they do not like the kind of decisions the judges are making.

This is all understandable, because we expect judges to make reasonable decisions for us, arising from their long experience of the law and the many different cases which come before them. They are paid to lift burdens from our shoulders. They get rid of doubts, where before there had been confusion and disharmony. When a judge listens quietly to a case, taking in all the facts and considering the law, if his judgment be right and fair and just the parties go away feeling freed of their problems. Even in criminal cases, where the defendant has been found guilty and has been sent to prison for many years, he will accept his sentence quite readily if he thinks he has had a fair trial and the judge has not been prejudiced against him. The prisoner knows that the sentence was right, and that he must serve his punishment in order to be re-united with society.

To become a judge requires long training in the law. In medieval times, such as the time when Sir John Fortescue wrote, the judges were chosen from a small number of lawyers called 'serjeants-at-law'. The word 'serjeant' has nothing to do with soldiers in an army: its real meaning, coming from the Latin, is 'servant'—'servants of the law'. So none of these men, however learned and important they might seem, forgot that they were servants. They started off by becoming 'apprentices of the law', from the French word *apprendre*, meaning 'to learn'. They could be learning the law for many years, before they were called to the degree and status of serjeant. And then there was a very impressive ceremony, involving the giving of gold rings, and much feasting, when they entered the 'brotherhood of the coif', as it was called. Becoming a serjeant meant that you had always to wear in public a white silk hood, which you never removed, even in the presence of the King. This was the coif. Nowadays, as we mentioned before, if you look closely at a judge's wig, you will see a small circle on top which represents the coif that the serjeants used to wear. And, even now, judges refer to other judges as their brothers, dating back to the time when Serjeants' Inn was a kind of hotel where they lived, dined and discussed together grave matters of law affecting the people.

The oath that serjeants swore on taking office required them to well and truly serve the people, to the best of their knowledge and ability, without counting the cost in terms of money. In the nave of old St Paul's Cathedral, before it was rebuilt following the Great Fire of 1666, each serjeant had a pillar by which he stood, available to be consulted by anybody, great or small, rich or poor. People could go to him and ask his advice; and there would be serjeants pacing up and down the wide, columned walk of the old church, discussing matters with their clients. If you were rich you would put money in the pocket of his gown; if you were poor you might not be able to afford anything. Nevertheless the serjeant had to hear you.

When you look at a barrister's gown today you will see that it has a black piece of cloth hanging from the left shoulder. This represents the pocket which used to hang behind, and into which money could be dropped, so as to avoid embarrassment to the wearer. It is meant to be a reminder that the barrister's gifts of intellect and speech were intended for the service of all, rich and poor alike.

In modern times the serjeants have become Queen's Counsel, senior barristers of long experience who wear silk robes when they attend court. If you ever go to the Royal Courts of Justice in the Strand, London, and wander into one of the courtrooms there, you will see, if you look hard enough, a little gate between the front row of seats and the other rows behind, on the aisle. The gate, or barrier, is always kept open; but, nevertheless, it marks off the court itself from the 'outer bar' or place where the public and their lawyers can come to be heard by the judges. An ordinary barrister is actually called an 'utter' or 'outer' barrister because he addresses the judges from just the other side of the little gate, called the bar of the court. Only Queen's Counsel or, in the old days, the serjeants, can stand and argue their case from inside the bar. This is because they are taken to have joined the brotherhood from which the judges are selected. They belong to the court itself.

All this sounds quaint and ancient, and not very practical today. In fact, today, the Bar is the name given to all the lawyers, called barristers, who have passed their examinations and are entitled to represent people in court. But the purpose of the little gate, or bar, is simply to remind people that, in the High Court, they are in the presence of Her Majesty the Queen doing justice through her own judges. The royal coat-of-arms is always just behind the seats of the judges.

This royal presence in the activities of the court is always most important. If you have a quarrel with somebody else, and you and your lawyers cannot patch it up, then sooner or later you will want to bring the matter before one of Her Majesty's judges for him to determine what is right for both of you. To bring the attention of the court to your problem, you will have to ask for a writ to be issued. This 'writ' is an old word, simply meaning writing. You put into writing the cause of your complaint and the law you are invoking to deal with the matter. Thus, if you have been run down by another man's car, you become the plaintiff and he becomes the defendant, and you state your claim in writing like this: 'The Plaintiff's claim is for damages for personal injuries and loss arising from the Defendant's negligent driving of his car at Cheapside, in the City of London, on or about the 12th day of December, 1983.' This gives very briefly—later it is expanded—the injury which he has done to you, and the fact that you want him to pay money damages to compensate you for (say) the loss of a leg, and the kind of law (in this case the law of negligence) which you think he has not regarded. It is always necessary to be able to put it down in writing, so that everyone can see whether you have a just cause of complaint.

Until quite recently the writ was a magnificent document. In Appendix C at the back of this book you can see what it looked like. Witnessed by the Lord High Chancellor, it is the command of the Queen that the defendant answers to the writ within a certain number of days, otherwise he might find judgment given against him. So, right from the beginning, the Queen is brought into the matter. This is because her peace has been broken by the dispute between you and the defendant: and the Queen's peace is the peace of the entire kingdom. The Queen, as the fountain of justice, will want to see that peace and harmony are restored between her subjects. You may think that, just because the other man drove badly (which he probably does not admit, and in due course will say you caused your own injury by charging out into the middle of the road), the Queen of all people is not concerned with such a relatively small matter. She must have a lot of greater problems to worry about! But you would be wrong: Her Majesty gave an oath at her Coronation that she would uphold the laws of the land, and if these laws appear to have been broken she is vitally concerned, through her judges.

This knowledge seem to have been lost, or ignored, recently. The form of writ which has replaced the document in Appendix C just says, in effect, 'please Mr So-and-so, we hate to trouble you, but there appears to be some difficulty between you and Mr Jones: would you tell us your side of the story?' It is all so nice and pleasant, but it misses the whole point of the exercise—which is, simply, that any dispute between people is not just between them, but the natural peace and harmony of the kingdom are threatened. The Queen comes into it, as the third point—the point to which everything in dispute can be referred—in order to re-unite the parties for the sake of the whole community. Whenever you have two people arguing with each other, it is nearly always best to bring in a third person whom they respect, and who will listen carefully to both sides, so as to restore unity. One-ness is really the natural state of people: if you have two people bitterly opposed to each other it is called 'duality', and that is no good, because it uses up their energies and talents; but introduce a third party who does not take sides and you have the opportunity to come back to oneness again.

In medieval times, according to the *Oxford English Dictionary*, the writ meant 'coming to the strength of the court'. It is like that. A good court, giving judgment based on reason, gives strength again, where before there was weakness produced by division between people.

A trial between two people is usually heard, in the first place, by a 'red judge', one of Her Majesty's Justices of the Queen's Bench, sitting in scarlet robes. But such is the care taken to get things right, and to re-unite people, that if either side is not satisfied that they have got justice or the right decision from the 'red judge' they can appeal to a Court of Appeal of three Lords Justices, sitting in black robes. And from here, with permission, a further appeal can lie to the House of Lords itself, the highest court in the land.

It is the same in respect of criminal matters. Great care is again taken, particularly because a decision of one of the criminal courts can mean someone going to prison for many years. First, there are magistrates' courts, in every town across the country. These deal with small crimes and they also decide, after hearing evidence, whether anyone accused of committing graver crimes should be sent to the Crown Courts for trial by judge and jury. Every English man and woman is entitled, except for petty crimes, to trial by jury if they are accused of doing something wrong. It is a very important safeguard, this trial by jury, because it means that the decision whether anyone is guilty or not guilty is left to twelve ordinary people and not to an officer of the state who might tend to favour the police. Usually the decision of a jury is final, but if anything goes wrong at the trial, or the judge states the law wrongly, there can be an appeal to the Court of Appeal, headed by the Lord Chief Justice of England; and from there, again, finally to the House of Lords.

Not always is everything in the court so serious and solemn as you might think, from the above account. Nor are judges always right, they are human both in their virtues and in their failings. Many writers have given us pictures of courtroom scenes, in which some judges have appeared bad-tempered and vindictive, particularly in the past. One of the most amusing scenes comes from Charles Dickens' *Pickwick Papers*, where poor Mr Pickwick has to appear in court to answer a charge made by Mrs Bardell that he had broken a promise to marry her. It all arose from a misunderstanding, but the good-natured Mr Pickwick does not get a very sympathetic hearing from the court:

> Mr Justice Stareleigh (who sat in the absence of the Chief Justice, occasioned by indisposition) was a most particularly short man, and so fat that he seemed all face and waistcoat. He rolled in upon two little turned legs, and having bobbed gravely

to the bar, who bobbed gravely to him, put his little legs underneath the table, and his little three-cornered hat upon it; and when Mr Justice Stareleigh had done this, all you could see of him was two queer little eyes, one broad pink face, and somewhere about half of a big and very comical-looking wig.

The judge had no sooner taken his seat than the officer on the floor of the court called out, 'Silence!' in a commanding tone; upon which another officer in the gallery cried, 'Silence!' in an angry manner; whereupon three of four more ushers shouted, 'Silence!' in a voice of indignant remonstrance . . . .

'Bardell and Pickwick,' cried the gentleman in black, calling on the case which stood first on the list.

'I am for the plaintiff, my lord,' said Mr Serjeant Buzfuz.

'Who is with you, brother Buzfuz?' said the judge. Mr Skimpin bowed, to intimate that he was.

'I appear for the defendant, my lord,' said Mr Serjeant Snubbin.

'Anybody with you, brother Snubbin?' inquired the court.

'Mr Phunky, my lord,' replied Serjeant Snubbin.

'Serjeant Buzfuz and Mr Skimpin for the plaintiff,' said the judge, writing down the names in his note-book, and reading as he wrote; 'for the defendant, Serjeant Snubbin and Mr Monkey'.

'Beg your lordship's pardon, Phunky.'

'Oh, very good,' said the judge; 'I never had the pleasure of hearing the gentleman's name before.' Here Mr Phunky bowed and smiled, and the judge bowed and smiled too; and then Mr Phunky, blushing into the very whites of his eyes, tried to look as if he didn't know that everybody was gazing at him—a thing which no man ever succeeded in doing yet, or in all reasonable probability ever will.

'Go on,' said the judge.

And on they went. Nervous Mr Winkle enters the witness-box to give evidence on behalf of Mr Pickwick and first gives his name:

'Winkle,' replied the witness.

'What's your Christian name, Sir?' angrily inquired the little judge.

'Nathaniel, sir.'
'Daniel—any other name?'
'Nathaniel, sir—my lord, I mean.'
'Nathaniel Daniel, or Daniel Nathaniel?'
'No, my lord, only Nathaniel; not Daniel at all.'
'What did you tell me it was Daniel for, then, sir?' inquired the judge.
'I didn't, my lord,' replied Mr Winkle.
'You did, sir,' replied the judge, with a severe frown. 'How could I have got Daniel on my notes unless you told me so, sir?'

This argument was, of course, unanswerable.

Not a very promising start for Mr Pickwick's case! In the end the jury find him guilty and he is ordered to pay Mrs Bardell £750 in damages. Do read it all some time, if you have a chance. It is very funny. Of course, Dickens himself had knowledge of the pomposity and shabbiness of the courts in the nineteenth century, and drew these word-pictures partly in order to get things changed.

6
Lawyers

> A lawyer is to do for his client all that his client might fairly do for himself if he could. —*Dr Johnson*

The work of lawyers—meaning judges, barristers and solicitors—is to take away from people the problems and burdens they carry around with them. Just as a doctor's gift of healing is meant to make people well again, so a lawyer works to heal the discords and rifts which appear in society. You may remember, from Chapter 1, that the very great lawyer, Sir William Blackstone, spoke of the law of God as meaning that all men should simply pursue their own happiness. That happiness, rightly understood, is the peace and bliss of their Creator. It is natural to men and women to be happy; therefore any unnatural things such as problems and worries ought to be removed. People can often solve their problems for themselves: but, when they cannot, they need to go to lawyers for advice and help. That is what is meant by Dr Johnson in the quotation at the top of this chapter.

So, in the first place, being a lawyer means belonging both to a vocation and a profession. A vocation simply means a calling—you have to feel inwardly that you would like to dedicate your life to this kind of service. And the word profession comes from the Latin, meaning 'to declare before all', 'to acknowledge publicly'. What is it that you declare and acknowledge when you become a lawyer? It must be that the law is there to protect people; to remove doubts, fears and confusion; and to lead them to freedom and happiness, if they will accept it.

The one thing that you cannot *make* people do is to become free. They will always find problems for themselves, if they really do not want to be free. Hence there is always work for lawyers! And, often, people have long ago given up their freedom because of the responsibility it carries with it: you have to observe the duties towards your neighbours if freedom is to work. The whole basis of the precious freedom which we enjoy in this country is the law of duties, which is the Common Law. So long as we observe good manners and are reasonable towards each other we shall enjoy freedom. You can see it in queues for buses: in this country we tend to wait patiently for our turn to board the bus and do not push and shove to get on. In other countries the attitude has long been, 'I don't want to know; I just want someone to tell me what to do and order me about'. The result has been, in Russia, for example, complete and utter slavery of the people.

There is a lovely story about freedom. A laundryman, who had a donkey to carry about his washing, fell ill and asked a neighbour to make his deliveries for him. The neighbour said he would. The laundryman told him where the donkey was and added, 'You don't have to untie the donkey. When he comes back at night just touch his hindlegs and he will think he is tethered for the night; and, in the morning, just touch his legs again and the animal will think he is free.' The story just illustrates the fact that we *think* we are either free or unfree, like the donkey. It is all to do with the mind. Problems and worries arise there; and it is the job of the lawyer to get rid of doubts and confusion and to give peace and certainty instead.

In medieval times the order of importance of the professions was said to be as follows: priest, teacher, doctor, lawyer. The priest was there to give spiritual comfort and to take away sins; the teacher's work was to remove ignorance and allow knowledge to flow; the doctor was under oath to maintain and preserve life; and the lawyer was concerned with people's liberty in society. What a magnificent order of service to mankind! Unfortunately, today, there is a tendency to get the professions backwards, with men and women more concerned about their possessions and their bodily health than with their spiritual welfare!

Even so, if you choose to become a lawyer, when you have been to university and passed the necessary examinations, you will have to be ready to serve the people who come to you for advice and help, and put them first, before your own convenience. They might be rich or poor, reasonable or unreasonable, angry or frightened: never mind, you will have to put aside your own likes and dislikes and serve them as faithfully as you can. It is a rule, for example, that a barrister who practises, say, in the criminal courts, cannot turn away instructions to appear for someone who is in trouble with the police, if he is not engaged on some other work. You cannot pick and choose your clients. Often you will hear people say, 'How could you possibly defend that man, who is a murderer, when you know he is guilty?' The answer is, you do not know he is guilty: every man is presumed to be innocent until he is *proved* guilty of the crime with which he is charged. It is not your task to judge him. Of course, if the man told you he was guilty, you could not mislead the court by pretending that he was not.

In 1840 there was a trial at the Old Bailey, the Central Criminal Court for London, of a man called Courvoisier who was charged with murder. Halfway through the trial, Courvoisier told the barrister who was defending him that he had, in fact, committed the murder. What was counsel (another name for barrister) to do? If it had happened before the trial began, no doubt the barrister would have told him that he could not represent him if he pleaded not guilty, or would have advised him to find another barrister. But this happened halfway through when, if counsel retired from the case, it would look very bad for Courvoisier. So the barrister went to get the advice of a judge who told him that he had to continue with the case, but that he could not suggest to the jury that Courvoisier was innocent: all he could do was to show up any weaknesses in the prosecution evidence and ask the jury whether they were sure, beyond reasonable doubt, that they could convict the prisoner on that evidence. The barrister went ahead and, in his final speech to the jury, he asked them to think long and hard before staining their hands 'with the blood of this young man'. This was in the days when men and women were hanged for murder. The jury retired and came back and found Courvoisier guilty. But counsel had done his duty, both by Courvoisier and the court: he had not misled the jury in any way, but had tested the evidence for the prosecution on whom rests the burden of proving their case in all criminal trials.

The first kind of lawyer that most people meet is called a solicitor. He deals with the public, helps them to buy and sell their homes, draws up wills and represents them in the lower courts. Often enough the advice and help a solicitor can give are all that is required to solve people's problems. The aim, after all, is not that people should go to court, but that they should agree amongst themselves what is right and what is wrong, or a conclusion that they can both accept, before starting on a long and expensive journey through the courts. The solicitor tells his client what the law is with regard to his or her particular problem, and often a satisfactory outcome can be reached.

But it may be that the parties still cannot agree, or that the law is difficult to understand. Then the solicitor may tell his client that a barrister should be instructed to advise in the matter. A barrister is often an expert in one or other of the branches of the law. In any event, the solicitor will want a barrister to represent the client in court, for barristers are trained to speak on behalf of people and they alone, not solicitors, can appear in the higher courts. Some people complain that it makes it more expensive to have two lawyers representing you, the solicitor and the barrister: but, in fact, it is often cheaper to do it this way, for the barrister's experience and knowledge of the courts will allow him to advise what the outcome is likely to be, and thus save money in the long run. It also makes sense that some lawyers, the barristers, are ready and keen to stand up and speak in public, while other lawyers, the solicitors, are more interested in meeting people and arranging their business matters for them.

It is a rule that barristers cannot meet the public directly: only through solicitors. A barrister cannot talk to a witness in the case, because he must not be seen in any way to try to influence what people will say in court. In criminal cases it would not do for the barrister to suggest a story that the accused person could tell in the witness-box, so as to provide him with a defence. And if a barrister should know of an 'authority'—that is, a case which was decided in the past by eminent judges and which would be helpful in guiding or directing the court in the present—he cannot sit quietly by and allow the court to arrive at a decision without the benefit of that authority, even if the authority is against his own argument to the court. He must never knowingly mislead the court.

On the other hand, counsel must speak fearlessly on behalf of their clients. They must not be overawed by judges who sometimes allow anger to sway their judgments. In the eighteenth century there was a famous barrister called Thomas Erskine. He had obtained from a jury a verdict which the judge, Mr Justice Buller, did not like. Here is part of the dialogue between Erskine and the Judge:

Erskine: I insist that the verdict shall be recorded.
Buller, J: Then the verdict must be misunderstood; let me understand the jury.
Erskine: The jury do understand their verdict.
Buller, J: Sir, I will not be interrupted.
Erskine: I stand here as an advocate for a brother citizen, and I desire that [the verdict given by the jury] may be recorded.
Buller, J: Sit down, Sir. Remember your duty or I shall be obliged to proceed in another manner.
Erskine: Your Lordship may proceed in what manner he thinks fit; I know my duty as well as your Lordship knows yours. I shall not alter my conduct.

The judge gave in. Indeed, he had to, because he was in the wrong and the barrister, Erskine, was right. The judge had tried to bully Erskine: but the duty of counsel is to be politely firm and courageous in the interests of the person he is defending. Judges from time to time do not like the verdicts brought by juries, but they have to accept them. That is why juries are so important to English liberty. Juries consist of ordinary men and women who, having heard all the facts and the law in a particular case, go away and between themselves decide whether the accused person is 'guilty' or 'not guilty' of the offence charged. They then come back into court and give their verdict, which is a word meaning 'saying truly'. Jurors are under oath to 'say truly' whether their fellow citizen shall be punished, or allowed to go free.

Lord Denning himself gives an example in one of his books of the personal courage which a barrister must have in defending a person charged with a crime, where the judge was unfortunately unfair in his conduct of the trial, and the jury of ordinary people did not like the judge's attitude and returned a verdict with which the judge did not agree:

> It was at Winchester Assizes, when a young sailor was charged with murder. He was said to have strangled a woman on Southampton Common. His counsel saw him in prison on the evening before the trial. He was dirty and unkempt and told his story. It was that the woman had slapped his face and said bitter things to him. He lost his temper and, to stop her talking, put his hands round her mouth and throat; but she had a weak chest and suddenly died. It was not a very strong defence. It is difficult to say that a slap on the face is sufficient provocation to reduce murder to manslaughter [i.e. killing someone but not with intent to murder]. Nevertheless his counsel felt it his duty to put it forward. He told the man to smarten himself up a bit before the next day. He did so. When he was brought into the dock [the place in court where the prisoner stands], he was as smart and nice a young sailor as you could ever wish to see. The judge did not think much of the defence. When counsel asked the sailor whether his ship had not been torpedoed under him three times, the judge intervened: 'Many a sailor has had his ship torpedoed under him, and doesn't go and strangle a woman.' When counsel put the defence of provocation to the jury, the judge said that he would rule that it was not open to the jury to find that there was sufficient provocation to reduce the offence to manslaughter. Despite this ruling, counsel felt it was his duty to put it before the jury. . . . But the judge directed the jury that he could see nothing to justify them in finding a verdict of manslaughter and that they must find a verdict of murder or

nothing. Now Hampshire juries have never been too subservient to the judges . . . and the jury, in flat contradiction of the judge's direction, found the sailor guilty only of manslaughter. The judge was very angry. He turned to the jury and said to them: 'Get out of the box [the jury-box or benches where the jury sit while they are in court]. You are not fit to be there. You have been false to your oaths.' They went but they had done their duty. The judge had to accept their verdict. He had indeed gone too far. As the jury left the court, they were heard to say: 'The judge was biased.'

Therefore there is a very great power in the barrister, through the use of his skill and his voice, to stand up for justice in society. He or she speaks for justice and the liberty of everyone. The barrister must know the law; must have a command of words; and must know how to speak well.

If you have seen *Rumpole* or *Crown Court* on television, you will know that part of the art of the barrister is to know how to ask questions. There are many rules about what questions you can ask. For example, they must be questions to do with the case being tried, and not just anything to confuse or annoy the witness. In dealing with a witness for your side of the case, you are not entitled to ask 'leading' questions: that is, questions which suggest the answers you would like to hear. In cross-examination, however, when you are dealing with a witness for the other side, you can ask leading questions—but you have to be careful because you might very well get an answer which destroys your own case. People sometimes say, 'Well, that's all right. The court should know the truth anyway.' But the point is that it is up to the barrister for the other side to get at the facts which support his case, and not for you to do his job for him.

In cross-examination the barrister hopes to get the witness for the other side to admit that he or she was wrong, or is not sure of the facts, or (if counsel knows that the witness is of bad character) that his or her evidence cannot be trusted. There are many examples of the effect of good cross-examination in the hands of very skilled counsel. One example comes from a case in which a brilliant young barrister appeared, called F. E.

Smith, later to become the Earl of Birkenhead and Lord Chancellor of England. Smith was representing a motorist charged with running down a young man, aged 19, who had lost the use of his arm through the incident. The young man's barrister had already asked him questions about how the accident occurred and what injuries he had sustained. The young man said he could not raise his arm any more and had shown the judge how painful it was just to raise his arm a little. Then came F. E. Smith's turn to cross-examine:

Smith: How old are you, young man?
Witness: Nineteen.
Smith: What games did you play before this accident?
Witness: Football and cricket.
Smith: And now?
Witness: I can't play either game now.

(So the witness has been put at ease by this kind of questioning. Then the barrister suddenly comes to the point:)

Smith: Dear, dear, how sad! And perhaps you would show us how high you could raise your arm *before* you had this terrible accident.

The young man raised his arm until it was above his head! All the barrister had to do then was sit down, saying to the Judge, 'My Lord will draw his own conclusions from that demonstration.'

Skill with words, and the ability to speak them well, in court, can only come through training and from a love of language. Sir William Blackstone, who spoke and wrote words so beautifully, loved to read Shakespeare when he was a young man. So it is always good practice to read widely, if you want to become a lawyer; and especially the great masters of language, such as Shakespeare. You may also want to hear how words rule, direct and guide men, through speeches such as those of Sir Winston Churchill—you can get his speeches on tape and on record. Also there is a very good cassette of Lord Denning speaking about law and his career, entitled *The Discipline of Law*.

If the idea of becoming a lawyer attracts you, and you would like to find out more about how to enter the profession, either as a solicitor or as a barrister, you will find set out in Appendix D of this book some basic information which will assist you.

We spoke earlier in this chapter of the duty of a barrister to put his own likes and dislikes aside and to speak for anyone who seeks his services. This happened to the barrister, Thomas Erskine. He was asked to represent Tom Paine, a troublemaker of the eighteenth century. Indeed, one judge went out of his way to warn Erskine not to appear on behalf of Paine: Erskine's own practice as a lawyer would suffer if it became known that he was willing to stand up for such men. But Erskine said it was his duty to appear, and he did. In his speech to the jury he said this:

> I will forever, at all hazards, assert the dignity, independence and integrity of the English Bar, without which impartial justice, the most valuable part of the English Constitution, can have no existence. From the moment that any advocate can be permitted to say that he will, or will not, stand between the Crown and the subject arraigned in the court where he daily sits to practise—from that moment the liberties of England are at an end. If the advocate refuses to defend, from what he may think of the charge or the defence, he assumes the character of the judge; nay, he assumes it before the hour of judgment; and, in proportion to his rank and reputation puts the heavy influence of perhaps a mistaken opinion into the scales against the accused, in whose favour the benevolent principle of English law makes all presumption, and which commands the very judge to be his counsel.

7
Torts

In this and the following chapters we shall look as the main areas of law with which lawyers are daily concerned. They are Tort, Contract, Property and Crime. Each is a vast subject in itself, so we can do no more than indicate the principles behind them. You will find, if you decide to study law, that the subjects come alive when you read cases decided by the judges in the Law Reports. For that you will need access to libraries specialising in law, or public libraries which have some of the Law Reports, such as the All England series or the Weekly Law Reports. There is an example in Appendix A of this book of the kind of judgment which is printed, showing the headnote, the reasons given by the judges for their decisions, and, most important of all, the facts of the particular case.

First of all, then, tort. The word, as we have already seen, in Chapter 1, comes from the Latin *tortus*, meaning twisted or wrong. So it is a wrong, a hurt or an injury done by someone to somebody else or to his property. Quite clearly, as Lord Atkin reminded us in the snail case, it is offending against the principle stated by Jesus, 'Thou shalt love thy neighbour as theyself'. In law that becomes you shall not injure your neighbour; and the question is, who is my neighbour?

What is the difference between a tort and a crime? If I come up to you and hit you in the face, so that your nose bleeds, you might very well report me to the police and they might advise you to go the the magistrates' court and obtain a summons against me for assault. If the case was tried by the magistrates, and I did not have a lawful defence, for example that I was only doing it because you attacked me first, I might be found guilty and ordered to pay a fine. That fine, a sum of money, would go to the State. You would have the satisfaction of knowing that I had been punished for my crime. But, supposing your nose had not stopped bleeding, and you had to go to hospital and perhaps have an operation, you could also go down to the County Court and issue a plaint against me for *damages* for the assault. That is, if you are over 18: otherwise you could get your parent or other relative to sue me as your 'next friend'. The damages, which are an award of money which the County Court Judge decides would put you back in the position you were in before you suffered the pain and injury and inconvenience of going to hospital, would be paid to you.

In the first case, the assault was a crime because it disturbed the Queen's peace; in the second it was a tort because it disturbed your peace. Everyone has this peace. It is the peace of body, mind and spirit which everyone needs to fulfil themselves and to express their talents for the good of society. The Queen's peace embraces the whole of society, and she is vitally concerned, through her judges, that this peace is not broken. Her Majesty's judges can punish me for my crime; and they can, in other courts, known as civil courts, order me to make compensation to you in money for the wrong I have done to you.

Historically, the beginnings of tort lie in trespass. This is a word we have met before, meaning 'passing across'. Usually we take trespass to mean going on to someone else's land without permission. But if you commit trespass by going on to someone else's land and at the same time you use force against him, his goods or his land, this would be trespass *vi et armis*: that is, by force and by arms. You have heard of the expression, 'An Englishman's home is his castle'. This can mean many things, including the fact that, from the earliest times of our history, we have always liked to live separately and apart from each other. But primarily it means that no-one, including a policeman or an officer of government, can enter our homes without our permission or without the lawful authority of a judge.

In medieval times people got fed up with their local lords

bursting into their homes, accompanied by armed men waving swords. They went to the King's Court for a writ of trespass *vi et armis* to prevent this kind of thing happening. The King was interested in securing justice in his own hands and he granted them this writ, for the King claimed that his peace now covered the whole of England, and it was not to be broken by the lords using force and arms.

The people liked that protection. Moreover, they wanted to extend it to cases where little or no force was used at all, where their goods were taken away from them, for example. In those days what was said in the writ, which commmanded the wrongdoer to appear before the King's Court, was all-important: you could not have a remedy if there was not a special writ designed to meet the wrong that was done. So people simply asked for a writ of trespass *vi et armis* even where no force or violence, in the strict sense, had been used. And the King's judges granted it, for cases where there had been interference with someone's bodily health, or goods, or land.

The English have always been very practical people. They have never liked being shut in by forms and procedures. If there are injustices, they will somehow get round the difficulties presented by the existing legal methods in order to cure the injustices. In their legal proceedings, the English have never minded inventing odd bits and pieces to help the cause of justice along: so, in the writ of trespass *vi et armis* they would simply claim that someone had taken away their goods, for which they wanted payment, and, as an afterthought, just to suit the writ, they would add words indicating that terrible force had been used, even where it had all happened quite peacefully. There used to be a character in English law called 'John Doe': he had never existed as a person, but everyone used him as a fictitious plaintiff or defendant. Poor John Doe regularly got kicked and beaten and thrown off his land, time after time in all the courts of the land, but no-one minded because he was just as unreal as Humpty Dumpty. You could do anything you liked with him. But, watching what happened to poor John Doe when he got to court, people interested in the outcome of the action knew what to expect, and could come to terms with each other.

However, even the judges balked at providing remedies under the writ of trespass *vi et armis* where the injury suffered was not direct, but happened later. For example, there was a case decided in 1726 in which one of the Judges said: 'If a man throws a log into the highway and in that act it hits me, I may maintain trespass, because it is an immediate wrong; but if, as it lies there, I tumble over it and receive an injury, I must bring an action on the case; because it is only prejudicial *in consequence*, for which originally I could have no action at all.' In the first example the judge gives it is assault because the injury received from the throwing of the log is a direct result; whereas, in the second example, men have a duty of care not to leave logs lying in the highway, when others can come along later and trip over them. Today we would call that negligence: but, in 1726, the judges were still searching for ways round the old, formal words used in the writ of trespass *vi et armis*. They had decided that, when circumstances arose when someone was injured later, such as tripping over a log which had been left in the road carelessly, he or she could have an 'action on the case' in which all that was necessary was to describe in the writ how the injury occurred, and who was to blame for it, and there would be no need to tie it down to a fictitious claim that the person had been assaulted 'with force and with arms'. Actions on the case therefore developed mightily in the King's Courts, since they offered freedom from the old, formal words of the writ.

Actually, Sir William Blackstone, sitting as a Judge of the Court of Common Pleas, with three other judges, did not exactly cover himself with glory when the case of *Scott* v. *Shepherd* came on for hearing in 1773. That was an interesting case in which a young man called Shepherd threw a lighted squib, made of gunpowder, from the street into a covered market. It was a most dangerous thing to do. The firework landed first on the stall of a man called Yates, who sold gingerbread. A quick-thinking man called Willis picked up the squib and threw it away before it could explode. It landed secondly on the stall of a man called Ryal, who again threw it away; and this time, unfortunately, it hit Scott in the face, exploding, and putting out his eye. So Mr Scott sued Mr Shepherd, in trespass, for damages for the injury to his eye.

The famous Blackstone said that he could not do that, he had got the wrong writ and the wrong action. Scott should have brought an 'action in the case' because his injury resulted not from the original throwing of the firework by Shepherd, but from Ryal later throwing it away, when it caught Scott in the face. But the other judges were having none of that: by that time they were not impressed by fine legal distinctions in procedures. They obviously thought that Shepherd must be made to pay for his carelessness, and they decided that the throwing of the squib between all the people involved was really one single act, starting with Shepherd who was, throughout, responsible for the damage. No doubt that was a just result, and Mr Justice Blackstone was overruled by the other judges.

In any event 'actions on the case', with their relative freedom from strict legal forms, gave rise to most of the modern torts, such as interference with goods, nuisance, and, above all, negligence. As we may recall, from our discussion of the snail case, Lord Atkin defined the modern law of negligence as follows: 'You must take reasonable care to avoid acts or omissions which you can reasonably foresee would be likely to injure your neighbour. Who then in law is my neighbour? The answer seems to be persons who are so closely and directly affected by my act that I ought reasonably to have them in contemplation as being so affected when I am directing my mind to the acts or omissions which are called in question.'

Another judge said, in the same case, that human relationships were always so different and so changing that no-one could define, once and for all, the kinds of duties which would arise between neighbours. In this he was stating that the Common Law, the law of duties, must always remain flexible and adaptable to all sorts of situations.

In fact, judges are always most careful to look back and be guided by what other judges have said in the past, before establishing rules to direct people's conduct in the future. This is because they do not want to divide people and make them angry and bitter towards each other, which might happen if opportunities were given to go to court at the drop of a hat. The aim is for men to live amicably together, and not let their squabbles bring them to court. So one golden rule in the law of torts is that you must have a legal right which is affected by someone else's conduct before you can bring your problem to the judges.

This can be illustrated by a case which was decided in 1929. In this case a small boy wandered onto land used by a coal mine. Lots of people used the land to walk over, and children for a playground, which was known to the mine-owners; but there was dangerous machinery present. It consisted of an engine and a large wheel for pulling cable from the pit. Tragically, the small boy was killed when the engine started up and hauled the cable along the ground. He could not be seen from where the engineer operated the levers. The judges said that the small boy had no legal right to be there, he was a trespasser on the land: which meant that the mine-owners had not given him permission. Since he had no legal right, his parents could not sue the mine-owners for the terrible injuries he suffered.

That might seem a harsh decision, particularly as the small boy would not have known what the word 'trespasser' meant! So, over the years following 1929, the judges worked to provide a legal right which children could have. Then, in 1972, nearly fifty years later, was decided *Herrington's Case* in the House of Lords, the highest court in the land. Again, a small boy was involved. He was playing in a field with his brothers. There was a path through the field leading towards an electric railway line. The railway line was fenced off, but the fence was broken down, a fact which was known to the British

Railways Board. They had done nothing about it. The boy climbed through the gap in the fence, went on to the line and was severely burned by the electric current.

The British Railways Board argued that the small boy had no right to be there, he was just a trespasser, and they could not be expected to owe a duty towards someone who was wrongly on the line. But judges looked carefully at the situation and noted that the Railway had, in fact, allowed the fence to remain in disrepair. They said that it was reasonably foreseeable that children would clamber through the gap. The child, who could not know what trespassing meant, had a legal right to be protected from the dangerous live rail on the Railway land. Accordingly, his parents could sue for the injury he had suffered through the breach of the Railway Board's duty of care.

Thus the law developed. In 1929, when the first case was decided, the judges had not had the advantage of Lord Atkin's famous statement in the snail case, about caring for one's neighbours. When that happened, in 1932, then the way was open for the development we have seen in the case of the small boy and the railway fence. Obviously the Railways Board and the small boy were neighbours, in the sense used by Lord Atkin, in that it was reasonably foreseeable that a broken fence offered no protection for children. In comparison with the boy the Railways Board were strong and quite able to spend money on keeping their fences in repair.

Well, you will say, all that is no consolation to the relatives of the boy who died in the mine accident in 1929, when the law was different and harsher, according to the judges. It is not actually a matter of the law changing: it remains the same. Everyone agreed with Lord Atkin when he said the law always was, and is, that you shall love your neighbour as yourself. It is just that, every so often, the law has to be re-stated by a very great judge in a form acceptable to the times in which we live. Sir William Blackstone may not have been right to decide against Shepherd in the squib case, on a technicality; but we owe to him, through his magnificent *Commentaries*, practically all we understand today about the very great principles of reason which underlie the Common Law of England. If we all, being human, sometimes lose our way, or forget, then we just have to be reminded about them.

That is all I want to say about tort, for the time being. There are many other torts which we have not discussed, except briefly, such as defamation, deceit and nuisance. But you will do well just to remember that torts are wrongs, done by some people towards others, for which the courts will award money damages in an attempt to put the injured person back in the position he or she was in before the wrong occurred.

8
Contract

Contracts happen all the time, so that we are hardly aware that they exist. They are really just bargains made between people. A bus pulls up at the bus stop: an offer is made to take us on a journey. We get on the bus and, by so doing, accept the offer and we are then legally liable to pay the fare. As you can see, a contract depends on both sides making a contribution to the bargain. The bus company agrees to take us on board its vehicle and transport us to our destination, and we, in return, agree to pay the price of a ticket.

Of course, you have to intend between you that a legally binding contract shall take place. If you got into your uncle's car and nothing was said about your helping to pay for the petrol, it would be assumed that it was simply a family arrangement, with no consequences to be determined in a court of law.

Offer and acceptance are therefore two essential factors in the making of a contract. You might think, looking at a shop window, and seeing articles marked at a particular price, that this was an offer to sell goods at that price: but the courts have held that the price tickets on goods are merely an invitation to you to buy, and that the offer part only takes place when you go up to the cash desk. You then offer to buy the goods at a particular price and it is up to the sales assistant whether or not to accept your offer. He or she can say 'Oh, I am sorry, but we got the wrong ticket on that coat. The price is really so-and-so.' It is then up to you to decide whether you will have the coat at the price quoted.

However, there are situations where an advertisement will be held to be an offer, not a mere invitation. This happens where the person offering cannot know whether the offer has been accepted until the other person has performed his part of the bargain. There is a case which every law student knows: if a law student does not know it, he or she cannot possibly expect to pass the examination in contract! Most law students complain that they cannot remember the names of the cases, to which they will have to refer in their examinations; but this case has a name which no-one can forget. It is called *Carlill* v. *Carbolic Smoke Ball Company.*

The company were the makers of a medicine, the carbolic smoke ball. They said in their advertisement that they would pay £100 to anyone who caught influenza after having sniffed their smoke ball for a certain period of time. Mrs Carlill bought one, sniffed away at it for the stated period, and caught influenza. She sued for the £100 and succeeded. She had accepted their offer, even though the company did not know who she was, had performed her part of the bargain and was entitled to the money promised.

Promises are very much part of the law of contract. The rule is, if you and someone else make promises to each other, you both have to carry them out. If the butcher promises to deliver meat next Monday, and you promise to pay him on delivery, and he does not turn up, you can sue him for a broken contract. The reason is that mutual promises make a bargain; and men must be held to the bargains they make. 'An Englishman's word is his bond' it is said. This is only partially true in law; you can make a promise to someone and, in law, it will only become effective as a contract if the other person does something, or promises something, in return.

The origins of the law of contract are to be found in the 'action on the case', which we discussed in the last chapter on torts. If a surgeon, for example, as happened in 1375, expressly undertook an operation on someone's hand, and made a mess of it, the injured party could sue him 'on the case'. This was called *assumpsit*, the Latin word meaning 'he undertakes'. In a later case, decided in 1602, the judges all declared that, each party undertaking to do a certain thing, the contract was formed simply from their mutual promises. This was quite different from the Roman Law which prevailed in

Europe, where a simple promise unsupported by anything done or said by the other party was sufficient to make a man liable. English law has always insisted on both parties contributing to the bargain to make them bound to each other, even if they just exchanged promises.

All this has to do with what is called 'consideration'. Consideration is a word which means thinking carefully about what you are going to do: so, in contract, the courts require some evidence that the bargain you entered into was not done lightly, but that it was sufficiently important to you for you to give up something of your own. Even a promise means that you intend fulfilling it in the future. Thus, if I promise to sell you my car for £1, I can be held to the bargain, even though the car is worth far more than that sum (I hope). The courts will not concern themselves whether it was a *bad* bargain: they will just want to see that *some* consideration was given by you to me, even though it was very little.

The doctrine of consideration requires that what you give up happens now or in the future, not in the past. You might have dug my garden for me last week; it will not do for me, a week later, to promise to pay you a sum of money for so digging it up. There is no contract, and you cannot sue me. The work was done without any promise as to payment having to be made. You made a gift of it to me. However, do not despair: you might be able to convince the court that, all along, there was an *implied* promise from me to you to pay for the work, otherwise you would not have done it. I have unjustly benefitted from all your labour, and the court might hold me liable under a *quasi-*contract (meaning 'almost a contract').

It is quite interesting to consider whether you, as a young person, under the age of 18, could be held liable on a contract. Supposing you went into a shop and bought clothes: could the shopkeeper sue you for the price of the clothes if, subsequently, you failed to pay? After all, you made use of the clothes; and they would not be much use to the shopkeeper after they had been worn. It would all depend on whether the clothes were *necessary* to you. In one case, decided in 1908, a young man, an undergraduate at Cambridge University (but still not an adult) went into a shop and ordered eleven fancy waistcoats. The tailor failed in his action to recover the money for the clothes because, the court said, he had not proved that the waistcoats were necessary to the undergraduate. It all seems a bit odd, because you would expect the tailor to think first before providing anyone with eleven such waistcoats, particularly an undergraduate. But perhaps he was thinking of a case decided in the nineteenth century when an Oxford jury held that champagne and wild ducks were necessaries to an undergraduate, and thus had to be paid for. Times have changed: and I doubt very much whether a court today would hold that champagne and wild ducks, or even fancy waistcoats, were necessaries as far as modern students at university are concerned!

This is why you will not obtain credit under the age of 18. Shopkeepers will accept cash from you, but they will not sell you items on credit for the simple reason that they might not be able to prove that the goods are necessary to your 'condition in life' and to your 'actual requirements at the time'.

However, a contract of employment is binding on you if it is to your benefit as a person under-age. The courts look at the contract itself to see whether advantage has been taken of your youth: if it has, the courts will probably release you from your bond. This happened in a case involving the famous showman and circus-master, Barnum. He hired a young girl to dance for him, and the terms of the contract were that he did not have to pay her if she did not dance (he could determine when and where); that he could send her abroad; and that she could not accept any other professional engagement, or marry, without his consent. The court held that the contract was unreasonably harsh and was invalid.

Contracts can be ended in a variety of ways, the best and most obvious being when both sides have fulfilled their parts of the bargain. This, of course, happens most of the time—otherwise there would be terrible confusion in society, and no-one would trust anyone else. If you look at textbooks of law, you would think that no contract ever was right: but this is because only the contracts which go wrong ever reach the courts. The others, the vast majority—which are mostly buying and selling goods and services—are completed successfully day by day.

Of course, if one of the parties to a contract breaks his promise, then the other party can treat the contract as at an end and can sue in the courts for damages. The damages will be a money award sufficient to put him in the same position as if the contract had been performed. This does not mean that the man who breaks the contract is liable for all the results of his failure, only those that were reasonably foreseeable at the time the contract was made. In a case decided in 1854, the owners of a mill in Gloucester hired someone called Baxendale to take a broken crankshaft back to the manufacturers in Greenwich, so that a new crankshaft could be made exactly the same as the old one. Mr Baxendale promised to deliver the broken pieces of equipment to Greenwich the next day. In fact he did not: the mill-owners did not get their crankshaft back until later than they expected, and they sued Mr Baxendale for the loss of their profits owing to the mill being out of operation that much longer.

The judge said: 'Where two parties have made a contract which one of them has broken, the damages which the other party ought to receive in respect of such breach of contract should be such as may fairly and reasonably be considered either arising naturally, i.e. according to the usual course of things, from such breach of contract itself, or such as may reasonably be supposed to have been in the contemplation of both parties, at the time they made the contract, as the probable result of the breach of it.' Applying that principle to the facts of the case, the judge held that Mr Baxendale was not liable for the loss of profit, while the mill was closed for the extra time caused by the delay in delivering the crankshaft, because Mr Baxendale had not been told that that might happen if he did not deliver on time; and because, in most cases, mill-owners would keep a spare piece of equipment in reserve for just such an emergency.

One of the other ways in which a contract can be ended is through frustration: in other words, through no fault of the parties contracting, a vital element disappears. This state of affairs can best be illustrated by what are known as the 'coronation cases'. When King Edward VII came to the throne his coronation was due to take place on a date in June 1902. Unfortunately, the King fell ill and the procession had to be cancelled. People had hired rooms overlooking the route of the procession and, of course, when it was cancelled they were disappointed. In some cases the landlords of the rooms sued in the courts to recover the rents which had been promised to them; but the courts held that the contracts had been frustrated, and any resulting losses had to lie where they fell, on both parties to a contract which could not be completed.

The principle of law which lies behind any contract is that both parties to the contract should know what they are doing. A bargain comes about through equality, that is, both parties must be taken to be fully aware of what each has and what each is willing to give up for the exchange to take place. This is all right where you have two big companies contracting with each other, one offering to buy and the other offering to sell a large piece of equipment. They ought both to have enough experts around to be able to tell whether the piece of equipment is good enough for the purpose required. But what about a contract made between an ordinary man or woman and a big company, where knowledge of what is being offered cannot be equal?

Centuries ago, when the law of contract was in its infancy, there was a strong principle about, going under the name *caveat emptor*—let the buyer beware. If you bought something, and the seller did not give you a warranty, or guarantee, as to its value, you were stuck with the item if it was not what it appeared to be. In 1603 a goldsmith, Chandelor, sold a precious stone to a man called Lopus for £100. He told Lopus that it was a bezoar-stone (which is a stone sometimes found in the stomach of an animal). Lopus afterwards discovered that it was not a bezoar-stone but a fake—but Chandelor did not know it. Lopus claimed damages. His claim was dismissed. The court said: 'Everyone in selling his wares will affirm that his wares are good, or the horse that he sells is sound: yet if he does not warrant them to be so, it is no cause for action.'

A famous historian once said that the movement of growth in society was from status to contract. What he meant by this was that, originally, society was based on status, where everyone knew his or her place in the scheme of things. You could be born into a family where it was almost certain you would become a soldier or a ruler; another family would give rise to churchmen, priests; another to merchants and makers of things; and by far the most children would be born into families which would have their own plots of land but which would be expected to serve the other orders of mankind. This was an ordered sense of existence, and it was firmly based on the duties you had to carry out, whether you were a priest, ruler, merchant or worker. You would find this kind of society in medieval times, going back about a thousand years or so. Contracts were not needed then, because the idea was that all provided for each other, the stronger protecting and cherishing the weak.

But with the coming of money and the desire to have more and more goods, the movement was away from the simple life of agriculture and few wants to a society concerned more and more with making things and exchanging them for money. The old order of simple duty began to slip away as men became greedy for goods. And ordinary people, who suffered poverty in the rush of a few men to make wealth, were expected to abide by the contracts they made, which were replacing the old order of duties from the strong to the weak. Nowhere was this more evident than in contracts of employment, where men, women and children were bound to harsh terms of working which they had to accept in order to live. Their land had been taken from them, and they were given, in return, low money wages or life in a grim prison called the workhouse.

We have seen in a previous chapter how Parliament had to intervene to control the number of hours worked under contracts of employment in factories, and the conditions under which men, women and children slaved. So it has been, ever since. Parliament and the courts have had to establish new duties and new controls over the kinds of contracts that ordinary people enter into, with big organisations and greedy individuals. Nowadays statutes made by Parliament to protect workers in their contracts of employment are so complicated and so strict that they are having the reverse effect, and making employers think twice before hiring people. Again, the law of contract which governs the relationship between landlords and tenants has become so complicated and so severe that it is very difficult for ordinary people to find rented accommodation at all. The courts have devised all sorts of fictions to get round the small print in written contracts which have worked injustices on people who have not the skill to understand them. In purchasing goods on credit, for example, there are many rules laid down to protect people whose desires have been inflamed and who think they cannot wait until they have the cash to pay for the goods.

So, the law of contract tends to become all the time more complicated. A wise man once said that if you wish to change the natural law, you will have to go on doing so, and making things more and more difficult. What is the natural law? You would probably find it working at its simplest and its best in a society where status is recognised, based on service from the strong to the weak, and where all provide for each other.

9
Property

Property is a fascinating area of the law. If you go to Lincoln's Inn, in London, and wander through the squares, with their lawns, you are in the home of Chancery lawyers who mostly deal with property matters. Outside the front doors of their chambers you will see long lists of their names written up, usually headed by Sir John This or Sir Robert That who are either eminent Queen's Counsel or judges sitting in the Chancery Division of the Royal Courts of Justice. Glance through the windows and you will see bundles of documents tied with pink ribbon, and shelves of old, leather-bound books extending up to the ceiling. It is all very quiet and courteous: not at all like the bustle which goes on in the Middle and Inner Temples, south of the Strand, where the Common lawyers live, hacking away at problems in crime, contract and tort.

It was in the Old Hall of Lincoln's Inn that the Lord High Chancellor of England sat, giving judgments in equity, which is a word meaning fairness or justice. If you remember, in Chapter 2, we looked at a description by Charles Dickens in his book, *Bleak House*, of the Chancellor sitting in a fog in the Old Hall and the case he was hearing grinding on for many long, weary years. All that has changed, and the conduct of the courts has become very much brisker, down in the Royal Courts of Justice in the Strand. But you can still see the lovely Old Hall in Lincoln's Inn where the Court of Equity sat for many centuries.

Although the lawyers here seem to spend most of their time delving into dusty old documents, they have on occasions to appear in court and, when they do, have often to speak up for liberty and principles of law. Their cases are by no means as dull and unexciting as they appear on the surface, because questions of property affect the lives and liberty of many people. All mankind depends on land for its food and its work. There is nothing made which does not come from the resources of the earth. And, in the end, when the articles made have served their purpose, they return to the earth. So, it is very important that the people have access to land, both to live on and to work on.

Sir Thomas More, whom we mentioned before, was a common lawyer by training, but a very great equity judge and Chancellor. In a book he wrote, called *Utopia*, he said that the cause of crime and stealing among ordinary people was the fact that, in Tudor times, they were being driven off their land to make room for sheep! For centuries families had been making their living from the land they worked and the cattle they kept in pasture; and now greedy landowners were driving them off, to replace them with sheep, which required very few people to look after them, but which gave handsome profits from the sale of wool for making into clothes. 'Noblemen and gentlemen,' said Sir Thomas More, 'yea, and certain abbots leave no ground for tillage, they enclose all into pastures; they throw down houses; they pluck down towns, and leave nothing standing, but only the church to be made a sheephouse.'

And where were they to go, the peasants forced from the land? 'They must needs depart away, poor silly wretched souls, men, women, husbands, wives, fatherless children, widows, woeful mothers with their young babes . . . away they trudge, I say, out of their own accustomed houses, finding no place to rest in.' No wonder, said More, that they resorted to stealing, in order to live!

The great Chief Justice Coke also wrote on the subject, later in the sixteenth century:

> Note, reader, that six inconveniences are introduced by subversion or conversion of arable land [land for growing crops] into pasture, tending to two deplorable consequences. (i) The first inconvenience is the increase of idleness, the root and cause of all mischiefs; (ii) depopulation and decrease of populous towns, and maintenance only of two or three herdsmen, who keep beasts, in place of great numbers of strong and able men; (iii) churches for want of inhabitants run to ruin, and are

destroyed; (iv) the service of God is neglected; (v) injury and wrong done to (priests); (vi) the defence of the land for want of men strong and enured to labour against foreign enemies, weakened and impaired. The two consequences are that these inconveniences tend (i) to the great displeasure of God; (ii) to the subversion of the policy and good government of the land, and all this by decay of agriculture . . .

Thus we have two of our most eminent lawyers and judges stating quite clearly that the causes of crime lie in the removal of people from their houses and land. Indeed, after they had spoken, matters got far worse, until, in the eighteenth and nineteenth centuries, there was no land left that the people could call their own and they were almost entirely dependent on any work that they could find in the misery of the factories. Parliament had to step in and, as we saw in the last chapter, try to regulate the hours and conditions under which men, women and, even, children, had to work. Even today we find that most people are dependent on working for big companies; and, if they lose their jobs, there is no land they can fall back on, in order to support themselves. They have to be supported by the state, through money payments known as 'unemployment benefits'. Ever since the land was enclosed by landowners to rear sheep the state has had to bring in 'Poor Laws' to alleviate suffering.

If you ever happen to fly over England in an aeroplane, and look down, you can see the present pattern of fields, with hedgerows and fences, like a huge jigsaw puzzle. That kind of pattern has only really grown up in the last two or three centuries: before, it would have seemed quite different. If you are lucky enough, and look closely enough, you might see the shape of a different system underlying the surface features of trees and fields of today. You might see what look like ripples running through the land. These are the marks of the medieval 'open fields' in which all the villagers had strips which they ploughed together. The ripples are the signs of the furrows. They shared the land; they grew their crops together; and they pastured their cattle on the common land.

Of course, today we should not be keen to go back to a simple life in which we all shared the hard work of growing our own food and looking after cows and pigs. We are all too ambitious for that. We all want the good things, such as cars and central heating and holidays in Spain. But a price has to be paid for all this: and the price is that we are dependent on those who own the land for access to it and for the ability to earn a living. Parliament has had to intervene on many occasions to ensure that land, privately held, is *used* for the good of the people.

In the last century there was a case in which a man called Pickles owned land through which ran streams, underground, which fed a reservoir owned by the City of Bradford. The reservoir was needed to supply water to all the taps in the city. The mayor and councillors of Bradford wanted to buy Mr Pickles' land to ensure that the underground streams would continue to supply the reservoir: but Mr Pickles, knowing what they wanted and being the owner of the land, simply asked too high a price. The City of Bradford could not afford it. So Mr Pickles stopped the streams from running from his land into the reservoir. It was sheer blackmail, in order to get as much money as he could. The mayor and councillors took him to court, but, unfortunately, the judges held that Mr Pickles could do what he liked with his own land, even it if caused suffering to others. Now, today, there are powers given by Parliament to local authorities, such as Bradford, to acquire the land which they need for public purposes, even from unwilling owners, at a fair price and not an extortionate one. Also, there are many planning laws which prevent people from using their land in a way which would offend others living nearby.

So the law of property really springs from the question, who owns the land? who owns the land of England?

In law, the owner of all the land of England is the Queen. You can ask your parents, who owns the house you live in? They might say that they pay rent to a landlord or to a local council; or they might say, we own the house. We have bought it and it is ours and no-one can take it away from us. We have what is called a 'freehold' and no-one has a better title to it than that. Of course, they are right: but you can surprise them with your knowledge and tell them what they have is a 'tenancy in fee simple absolute in possession'. At this stage they might well look puzzled, so you will have to explain. The word 'tenancy' means 'holding', so that, in the first place, they hold the land from the Queen. Not only the land itself, but the house which is built on it; for a sale of land will include all that is fixed to it and all that is above and below it. As Chief Justice Coke said, 'the earth hath in law a great extent upwards, not only of water . . . but of air and all other things even up to heaven.' So that if a builder swings a crane jib through the air over your property, he is trespassing unless you have given him permission. But do not try to prevent aeroplanes crossing over your property: Parliament has decreed that they can!

Next, you can tell your worried parents that the word 'fee' simply means that they can leave title to the land to you in their wills, after they die; and 'simple' means what it says, there are no conditions attached. The words 'absolute in possession' just signify that, at the end of the day, your parents have a better right than anyone else to stay there.

Now we can say much more exactly what it is your parents *do* own. The Crown owns the land itself. What your parents have is *time* in the land: they own an *estate* in the land, called the fee simple estate, which entitles them to use the land for an indefinite time, and to pass it on after their deaths. But if, for example, you and your family all disappeared, and there was no-one to claim the fee simple estate, then ownership of the land itself would still remain with the Queen.

This is a very meaningful word, 'estate'. It comes from the little Sanskrit word *stha*, meaning 'to stand', which gives rise to so many important words in our language, like statute, status, estate, statue: all to do with men's standing and *how* they stand, and *where* they stand. The freehold estate, for example, is the holding of a free man: that is, in the old days, the measure or *status* of a free man was that he had the longest time to enjoy the land he and his heirs lived on. But, having invented this extremely useful piece of fiction called an estate, English Common Law then allowed the owner of it to grant to others periods of time over which they could use the land itself: your parents could, for example, grant the use of your house to someone else for the period of the rest of their life, or for a term of some years, or even for a time which does not start until some future event. It is very flexible and allows all sorts of interests to arise, out of the indefinite period of time during which your parents have the freehold. Meanwhile, the Queen continues to be the owner of the land itself.

It is also possible to put the freehold estate 'in trust'. This is another useful piece of fiction, invented by English law, by which the legal owners of a particular estate can be one group of persons, and the true owners are other people. The legal owners are called 'trustees' and the true owners are 'beneficiaries'; and the rules of equity, or conscience, require the trustees always to act in the interests of the beneficiaries. The trust can work very well, for example, where some of the beneficiaries are children who do not know the ins and outs of dealing in property.

In Anglo-Saxon times the King was trustee of the land for the people. The true owners were the people. They called it 'folk-land'. But, when William of Normandy conquered England in 1066, he had other ideas: he said that the land, by virtue of its conquest by him and his knights, belonged to the Crown. He granted estates in the land to his chief followers, who had supported him in the battle. He said that all land was to be held and used in return for services: thus, the service of the barons to the King was rewarded by large chunks of land; and each of the barons was entitled to allow others the use of parts of his land in return for personal services to him. This went all the way down to the peasant, who had to do personal service to the lord of the manor, like ploughing his land and gathering his crops, in return for the use of some strips of land in the big open fields.

This was called the 'feudal system' and what it meant was that ordinary men and their families could no longer move around from place to place, but were tied to one lord whom they served and who allowed them the use of land in return. Sir Winston Churchill describes it in his great book, *History of the English-speaking Peoples*:

[in Anglo-Saxon England] the idea still persisted that the tie of lord and man was primarily personal, so that a free man could go from one lord to another and transfer his land with him. The essence of Norman feudalism, on the other hand, was that the land remained under the lord, whatever the man might do. Thus the landed pyramid rose up tier by tier to the King, until every acre in the country could be registered as held of somebody by some form of service.

And Shakespeare has the dying John of Gaunt say to King Richard II: 'Landlord of England art thou now, not king.' He meant that, by the time of Richard, in the fourteenth century, estates in land were being bought and sold, and rented out for money, with very little reference to the interests of the people themselves.

John of Gaunt says, in a famous speech about England:

> This land of such dear souls, this dear, dear land,
> Dear for her reputation through the world,
> Is now leased out—I die pronouncing it—
> Like to a tenement, or pelting farm:
> England, bound in with the triumphant sea,
> Whose rocky shore beats back the envious siege
> Of watery Neptune, is now bound in with shame,
> With inky blots, and rotten parchment bonds:
> That England, that was wont to conquer others,
> Hath made a shameful conquest of itself.

In the eighteenth century, Sir William Blackstone wrote in Volume II of his famous *Commentaries*:

> There is nothing which so generally strikes the imagination, and engages the affections of mankind, as the right of property; or that sole and despotic dominion which one man claims and exercises over the external things of the world, in total exclusion of the right of any other individual in the universe. And yet there are very few that will give themselves the trouble to consider the original and foundation of this right. Pleased as we are with the possession, we seem afraid to look back to the means by which it was acquired, as if fearful of some defect in our title: or at best we rest satisfied with the decision of the laws in our favour, without examining the reason or authority upon

which those laws have been built. We think it enough that our title is derived by the grant of the former proprietor, by descent from our ancestors, or by the last will and testament of the dying owner; not caring to reflect that (accurately and strictly speaking) there is no foundation in nature or natural law, why a set of words upon parchment should convey the dominion of land; why the son should have the right to exclude his fellow-creatures from a determinate spot of ground, because his father had done so before him; or why the occupier of a particular field or of a jewel, when lying on his death-bed and no longer able to maintain possession, should be entitled to tell the rest of the world which of them should enjoy it after him.

But, later in the same chapter, after he has discussed the fact that in the early ages of mankind, the land was held in common and everyone took from the public stock to his own use such things as he required, Blackstone goes on to say:

> But when mankind increased in number, craft, and ambition, it became necessary to entertain conceptions of more permanent dominion; and to appropriate to individuals not the immediate *use* only, but the very *substance* of the thing to be used. Otherwise innumerable tumults must have arisen, and the good order of the world been continually broken and disturbed, while a variety of persons were striving who should get the first occupation of the same thing, or disputing which of them had actually gained it.

So you can see from the above how important the law of property is, in terms of our fundamental freedom. Whatever the past history of the subject, there is always need for a law which establishes, with reasonable certainty, what is and what is not our property, in order to free people from the burdens of constantly disputing with each other over their material possessions.

10
Crime

If you go to Madame Tussaud's waxworks museum, in London, you may see, in the Chamber of Horrors, all sorts of ways in which people were punished for committing crimes, in the past. They range from gallows to guillotine, which was a heavy knife that descended between rails to cut off the heads of unfortunate victims strapped below. There are waxwork models of infamous murderers: and, all in all, there is a kind of gory fascination about the methods of torture and execution on display.

In this country, capital punishment has been abolished by Parliament, which means that no-one can be sentenced to death by a court, even for very cruel crimes. But they can be sent to prison for a very long time, perhaps even for the rest of their lives. In the days when men and women could be sentenced to death for murder, the judges, in pronouncing sentence, would put on a black cap and would say, 'You shall be taken from here to the prison and from there to the place of execution and there you shall be hanged by the neck until you are dead: and may the Lord have mercy on your soul.' There would be a chaplain in court, and he would say 'Amen'.

So the one thing you can say about crime is that it is conduct which, when detected, leads to punishment by the state. We discussed, in Chapter 7, the kinds of wrongs which people can do to each other which result in the courts ordering the wrongdoers to pay money damages by way of compensation. But there are wrongs which the state itself cannot excuse and which it will punish both for the sake of the offender and as an example and warning to others. Murder, for example, is such a terrible crime that the state requires a sentence of life imprisonment to be passed on anyone who is convicted of killing another, with intent to kill him or her or to inflict very serious injury. The hope is that the murderer will redeem himself through severe punishment, when perhaps he can be released on licence or parole in the future. Similarly, if someone commits robbery, which means stealing with the use or threat of violence, he can expect a long term of imprisonment.

The reason is that the Queen's Peace has been disturbed. The Queen's Peace extends over all the country, and includes us all. We each have our own peace which, under English law, is very highly valued; and we saw, in Chapter 7, how watchful the Queen is that peace should be restored between people who bring their complaints before the court. The word 'peace' probably comes from a Sanskrit word *pas* meaning 'to bind'. Men are bound together, in harmony, when they are at peace; and divided from each other when they are at war. Thus the Queen's Peace binds us all together. In the Crown Courts, which deal with criminal offences, an indictment is a document which tells the defendent precisely what he or she is accused of doing; and the indictment often includes the words, 'contrary to the peace of our Sovereign Lady, the Queen'.

The indictment is such an important document because no-one must be deprived of his or her liberty without being told precisely what crime is alleged, and on evidence from which the jury can be sure of his or her guilt. When a policeman arrests anybody he must say what it is he suspects that person has done. He also tells the person, 'You are not obliged to say anything unless you wish to do so but what you say may be put into writing and given in evidence'. Here, again, the law is protective of individual liberty, because you do not have to say anything, either then or later when you appear before the court. It is the Queen who alleges that you have broken her peace, and it is up to her, through her prosecuting counsel, to prove the charge against you.

Everyone is innocent until proved guilty.
One Lord Chancellor described it as follows:

Throughout the web of English Criminal Law one golden thread is always to be seen, that it is the duty of the prosecution to prove the prisoner's guilt . . . If, at the end of and on the whole of the case, there is a reasonable doubt, created by the evidence given by either the prosecution or the prisoner, as to whether the prisoner killed the deceased with malicious intention, the prosecution has not made out the case and the prisoner is entitled to an acquittal. No matter what the charge or where the trial, the principle that the prosecution must prove the guilt of the prisoner is part of the Common Law of England and no attempt to whittle it down can be entertained.

So it is the Queen who prosecutes someone for having broken her peace, through Counsel for the Crown in a criminal trial; and it is for the Crown to prove guilt, not for the accused subject to prove his or her innocence. But the mystery then deepens: for it is not only the Queen who prosecutes, but it is the Queen, through Her Majesty's Judges, who presides over the trial and gives sentence when and if the accused is found guilty. How is this, that the Queen can both bring the charge and judge it? Is that fair and just? For there is another rule which says that no-one shall be a judge in a cause to which he is a party: *nemo debet esse judex in propria sua causa*, as the Latin maxim says.

The answer is, that though the judges are the Queen's Judges, they are quite independent of her, and cannot be dismissed if they find against the Crown and for the subject. The most senior judges hold their appointments until retirement, and can only be removed by both Houses of Parliament acting together if their behaviour is very bad indeed.

There was a King, James I, who tried to take matters into his own hands and judge them for himself: but he was told, in no uncertain fashion by the judges of the time, foremost among them Chief Justice Coke, that 'no king after the Conquest, assumed to himself to give any judgment in any case whatsoever which concerned the administration of justice within this realm; but these were solely determined in the

Courts of Justice'. In other words, the judges were not going to let the king decide cases in which the King himself had an interest: they were to be decided by the judges themselves, who would show fear or favour to no-one. It took a good deal of courage to tell King James this, because he was a grim old monarch who did not take kindly to any opposition.

But the point at issue was a very fundamental one, as far as the judges were concerned. In about 1250 the lawyer, Bracton, had stated: 'The king must be under no man, but God and the law, for the law makes the king'. This is the basis of our government and our freedom in this country, because what it means is that the King, or Queen, and all who serve him or her, as Ministers or Civil Servants or, even, policemen, can only act in accordance with the Common Law and Statute Law accepted by the people. If they step outside these laws, or try to make regulations of their own, they can be stopped: and it is the independent judges who will stop them.

Sometimes in the Law Reports you will see the name of a case which goes something like this: 'Regina (Queen) against Secretary of State for Home Affairs, ex parte Smith'. What does it mean? The Queen in dispute with one of her own Ministers—how can that be? And who is this chap, Smith, who creeps in at the end? Actually what has happened is that Mr Smith claims that the Secretary of State has done something wrong to him, and he invokes the Queen's name to bring the Minister before the court. Then the judges will have to decide between the interests of the government and those of the subject, Mr Smith. The judges will have to bear in mind the oaths they have sworn, to 'do right to all manner of people after the laws and usages of this Realm without fear or favour, affection or ill-will'.

What is it that the Queen, through Counsel for the Crown, has to prove in order to satisfy a jury that someone is guilty of the crime with which has or she has been charged?

The law requires two things to come together for any crime to be committed: a guilty mind and a guilty act. Lord Chief Justice Kenyon said, in 1789: 'It is a principle of natural justice, and of our law, that *actus non facit reum nisi mens sit rea*.

The intent and the act must both concur to constitute the crime.' You cannot charge anyone with murder if they did not *intend* to kill the victim, or to do him some really serious injury.

But how can you prove, to the jury's satisfaction, that anyone actually intended to commit a crime? As the judges sometimes say, you cannot lift off the top of the accused's head and look inside and see whether there was a guilty intention somewhere in his mind. It is then that the jury have to use their common sense. They must look at all the facts of the case, and at what was said and done by the accused, to see whether it has been proved that he or she had the necessary intent. If some men are seen with guns in their hand, threatening a bank guard and snatching the money bag from his hand, and then they try to escape, it probably would not take a jury long to decide not only that they were caught in the guilty act but that they actually intended to commit the crime of robbery. Of course, not always it is as simple and direct as that: if you look back at Chapter 6 you will find there the story of one case, told by Lord Denning, in which a young sailor's defence was that he never wanted to kill the young woman on Southampton Common, but she had taunted and provoked him and, in the heat of the moment, he had put his hand round her throat. She had a weak chest, and died. The jury listened to all this; heard the young sailor give his evidence; heard the speeches of Counsel for the Crown and for the Defence; watched how the judge dealt with the matter; and decided that, although the killing was unlawful, it was not done with intent to murder.

Thus, the jury is of great importance in a criminal trial. They have to decide on a verdict of guilty or not guilty. The accused person is put in their charge, and only they can say, having heard all the evidence and watched the witnesses, whether the charge has been proved to their satisfaction, or not. When someone is tried before a jury, he or she is said to be 'put on their country', because the jury represents the country. Twelve ordinary people, selected at random, sit in judgment on the accused; and, even though the judge directs them as to the meaning of the law applied to the facts of the case, there is nothing to stop any jury returning a verdict of not guilty if they do not like the law itself, or think it harsh or unreasonable— as they did in time past, when people could be hanged for stealing sheep. There was a certain grim irony in this, because, as we saw in the last chapter, it was those very sheep which had forced men to leave their land! And juries would not convict: they knew what the penalty was, and they thought the law was oppressive.

Sir William Blackstone goes so far as to say that trial by jury in the 'grand bulwark' of an Englishman's liberties. That is, his freedom is protected by the necessity of proving serious charges against him in front of a jury made up of people just like him. Blackstone points to what was said in Chapter 39 of Magna Carta, the great declaration of freedom which was secured from King John in 1215:

> No freeman shall be arrested, or detained in prison, or deprived of his freehold, or outlawed, or banished, or in any way molested; and we will not set forth against him, nor send against him, unless by the lawful judgment of his peers and by the law of the land.

The word 'peers' means 'equals'. The House of Lords is sometimes called the House of Peers, but that is simply because the lords are the equals of each other. So a jury is said to be made up of a man's peers.

Blackstone goes on to say:

> So that the liberties of England cannot but subsist, so long as this *palladium* remains sacred and inviolate, not only from all open attacks, (which none will be so hardy as to make) but also from all secret machinations, which may sap and undermine it; by introducing new and arbitrary methods of trial, by justices of the peace, commissioners of the revenue, and courts of conscience. And however *convenient* these may appear at first, (as doubtless all arbitrary powers, well executed, are the most covenient) yet let it be again remembered, that delays, and little inconveniences in the forms of justice, are the price that all free nations must pay for their liberty in more substantial matters; that these inroads upon this sacred bulwark of the nation are

fundamentally opposite to the spirit of our constitution; and that, though begun in trifles, the precedent may gradually increase and spread, to the utter disuse of juries in questions of the most momentous concern.

Since Blackstone's time, the jury has largely disappeared from the civil courts where questions relating to tort, contract and property are tried; but they continue to exist in the Crown Courts where criminal charges are brought. Justices of the peace, or magistrates, sit in towns all over the country, and they are allowed to deal with small crimes, if the accused person agrees: but if he or she insists on being tried by a judge and jury then, in most cases, the matter must go up to the Crown Court. From time to time you will hear people in authority complaining about this right to trial by jury because, they say, it costs the state a lot of money to have matters tried in the Crown Courts when magistrates could deal with them, especially thefts of small sums of money or a few items from local stores. But, of course, this is precisely what Sir William Blackstone warns us against: that if you take away the right to jury trial in trifling matters, gradually the practice will spread, until you lose it in 'questions of the most momentous concern'. And who is to say whether a crime is trifling to the person who is charged with it? A man or woman, who has never been in trouble with the police before, and who is wrongly accused of taking a few items from a store, will want the fullest and best hearing in order to clear his or her name. People can lose their jobs and their friends if they are convicted of dishonesty.

Juries are independent and they are impartial. They do not take sides. They do not support the prosecution or the defence. They listen to all the evidence and are directed on the law by the judge. They then go away, by themselves, in private, and decide whether they are satisfied, so that they are sure of the accused person's guilt. If they are left with a reasonable doubt, then they must return a verdict of 'Not Guilty'.

It used to be required that the only verdict which a judge could accept from the jury was one on which all twelve men and women had agreed—either guilty or not guilty. Then

Parliament changed the law, so that, after long deliberation, a jury could be permitted to bring in a verdict on which a majority of ten had agreed. It could not be less than ten. It is a pity, in a way, that this was done: and is an example of the unthinking way in which old methods can be upset, without the knowledge of why it was done like that in the first place. Many men and women who have served on juries will tell you that they have enjoyed the experience, and have found that, while on a jury, it took on a life and being of its own. They felt as if they had become part of a larger body than their own, with its own mind, feelings and opinions. The jury was a body quite capable of reaching its own decision, quite separately from the individual views of its twelve members. If you ever have a chance, there is a film worth seeing, called *Twelve Angry Men*, in which a whole jury changes its mind during the course of a long afternoon. If, of course, the jury could not finally agree on a verdict, then another jury would have to hear the case.

Now that has been changed, and the change has resulted in divided juries, rather than juries speaking with one voice. It is clear that Parliament did not understand what it meant to serve on a jury and become part of a larger mind and body. Yet, for most people who are called for jury service, it is the one opportunity in their lifetimes actually to participate in the government of their country.

Blackstone calls the jury a bulwark of our liberties. 'Bulwark' is a lovely word, and it means a powerful defence. As long as we have juries, therefore, we have a powerful defence against forces which would reduce our liberties and freedom. But freedom itself is watched over and stated by the judges: they are the men who ultimately keep us free. And we always need judges who state firmly and fearlessly what the law is.

We have spoken before about one of our very greatest of judges, Lord Atkin. In 1941, when a great war was raging, and the prospects for Britain looked dim, Lord Atkin and four other Law Lords had to decide a famous case, called *Liversidge v. Anderson*. Sir John Anderson was the Home Secretary at the time—in other words, the King's Minister responsible for the police and for all matters relating to security. There was a great fear about that certain people's loyalty could not be trusted, and that they would spy or help in some way Hitler's Germany to win the war. So Parliament had given the Home Secretary wide power, just while war lasted, to detain suspected persons and put them in prison without a trial. However, the regulation passed by Parliament was in these words:

> If the [Home Secretary] has reasonable cause to believe any person to be of hostile origin or associations . . . and that by reason thereof it is necessary to exercise control over him, he may make an order against that person directing that he be detained.

Mr Liversidge was just such a person, it was claimed, and he was put in Brixton Prison. But the Home Secretary would not tell him *why* he had been put there, or what it was he was supposed to have done. No-one could tell whether the Home Secretary had 'reasonable cause' or not. When you have the word 'reason' or 'reasonable' in a statute, it usually means that someone has to give his reasons for acting in a certain way, and then the judges can say whether those reasons are good ones, or not. Courts of Law are reasonable places; and it is the function of judges to determine right and wrong in the light of reason. And one must never forget the fundamental principle of our constitution, that the King (and all who serve as officers of state) must be under no man, but God and the law, for the law makes the King. Getting Ministers to state their reasons before a Court of Law is one way of ensuring that they always act within the law, and not according to their own whims and fancies.

But the Attorney-General, the King's Officer, argued in the House of Lords that the Home Secretary's act in taking away the liberty of Mr Liversidge could not be called in question in a Court of Law. The reasonableness of his conduct was a matter for the Home Secretary alone. In effect the Attorney-General argued that the words in the regulation 'If he has reasonable cause' meant if the Home Secretary *thinks* he has reasonable cause. All the other judges went along with that argument, because, they said, war-time was an exceptional situation. But not Lord Atkin. He said:

> ...In this country, amid the clash of arms, the laws are not silent. They may be changed, but they speak the same language in war as in peace. It has always been one of the pillars of freedom, one of the principles of liberty for which on recent authority we are now fighting, that the judges are no respecters of persons and stand between the subject and any attempted encroachments on his liberty by the executive, alert to see that any coercive action is justified in law. In this case I have listened to arguments which might have been addressed acceptably to the Court of King's Bench in the time of Charles I.

(The meaning of this is that Charles I, like his father King James, thought that he was all-powerful and could use the law for his own purposes.)

> I protest, even if I do it alone, against a strained construction put on words with the effect of giving an uncontrolled power of imprisonment to the minister. To recapitulate: the words have only one meaning. They are used with that meaning in statements of the common law and in statutes. They have never been used in the same sense now imputed to them ...
> I know of only one authority which might justify the suggested method of construction. 'When I use a word,' Humpty Dumpty said in a rather scornful tone, 'it means just what I choose it to mean, neither more or less.' 'The question is,' said Alice, 'whether you can make words mean so many different things.' 'The question is,' said Humpty Dumpty, 'which is to be master—that's all' ... After all this long discussion the question is whether the words 'If a man has' can mean 'If a man thinks he has'. I am of opinion that they cannot, and that the case should be decided accordingly.

Recognised as he was as a very great judge, Lord Atkin did not make himself popular with his fellow Law Lords when the words above were uttered. But popularity did not matter. The law had to be stated, and maintained, fearlessly. And it is significant that no-one now remembers what the other judges said, but they do remember and cherish Lord Atkin's words. It is now accepted that what he said was the law is correct. As for Mr Liversidge—he was released from prison shortly after!

Epilogue

This book is about law, and about freedom. Freedom does not mean doing what you like, when you like. Freedom itself can only be found through law: the 'dom' part of the word is 'doom', our old English word for law. 'Free' means 'friend, dear one'—so it is the law of friends.

I hope you have enjoyed the book and that you will continue to be interested in law, especially Common Law. There is much to read on the subject, most of it, I'm afraid, very technical. But a lawyer should always be someone who has read widely and who loves words. There is no better training than to read the great poets, statesmen and lawyers of the past: Shakespeare, Blackstone, Burke and, probably above all, Plato, the philosopher who gave us the foundation of our freedom.

We need to know about our rich heritage of law, language and liberty. Unless we do know about it, and the reasons behind it, we shall lose it all, simply through ignorance.

HRH The Prince of Wales said recently: 'Law in our society and the legal framework, built upon and improved throughout the centuries in Britain and adopted by other countries such as Canada has preserved our freedom as individuals. The administration of a system of law by an independent judiciary which is seen to establish the equality of all before that law, is the means by which our democratic way of life can exist and be preserved.' The Prince went on to say: 'We have an increasing obligation to concentrate on developing our moral courage and a corresponding awareness of that inner force that we all possess.' The inner force, he said, comes from the overwhelming strength of human spirit and the power of faith.

So there is much to read, much to learn, and much to put into practice. But is is all such *interesting* work, understanding principles of law and seeing how they apply in the modern world.

Good luck with your studies!

Appendix A: A Common Law Judgment

(1957) 1 All E.R.583 ← Name of the Law Report / Name of Plaintiff

BEHRENS AND ANOTHER v. BERTRAM MILLS CIRCUS, ← Defendent
LTD

[QUEEN'S BENCH DIVISION (Devlin, J.), December 3, 4, 5, 6, 7, 13, 14, 17, 18, 19, 21, 1956, January 30, 1957.] ← Dates when case tried

Animal—Liability for keeping dangerous animals—Elephants—Burmese circus elephants frightened by barking dog—Dog illicitly brought into fun fair booth by licensee without knowledge of circus owners—Booth knocked down by elephants—Midgets inside booth injured—Elephants not acting viciously—Whether circus owners liable for damages.

Damages—Mental shock—Fun fair booth knocked down by elephant—No physical injury to plaintiff who was inside booth—Whether damages recoverable for shock.

Damages—Measure of damages—Loss of joint earnings—Husband and wife performing midgets—Act not joint one, but husband exeptionally dependent on wife—No work done by husband during wife's incapacity although husband fit to work—Whether husband entitled to damages in respect of loss of half the joint earnings during period of wife's illness.

Areas of law covered in this case

The defendants held a circus each year for which they rented part of a building. A fun fair was run in conjunction with the circus, in the same premises, and while the defendants retained general control over the fun fair, they granted licences to amusement caterers to provide entertainment there. W. held a licence from the defendants to set up a booth in the fun fair in which the two plaintiffs, who were midgets and were husband and wife, were exhibited. The plaintiffs put up half the money for the booth and took half the takings. The booth was situated in a corridor which led from the circus to the main part of the fun fair, beyond which the defendants had a

THE HEADNOTE (brief description of facts and decision of the judge)

94 Young People's Book of Law

menagerie where they kept six Burmese elephants who performed in their circus; to reach the circus, the elephants had to pass along the corridor where the booth was. Neither W. nor the plaintiffs knew, at the time when the licence was granted, that elephants would be passing their booth. On the day in question, W. had a small dog with him in the booth, although it was the defendants' rule that animals were not allowed into the circus or fun fair. When the elephants came along the corridor the dog ran out from the booth barking, and frightened one of them who went after the dog in the direction of the booth followed by another elephant. As a result, the booth was knocked down by the elephants and the plaintiff wife who was inside with her husband was seriously injured. Her husband, although not physically injured, suffered a considerable shock and went to bed for a week after the accident; thereafter he was fit to work.

The earnings of the plaintiffs were paid to them jointly, their expenses were paid jointly and the benefit of their earnings was shared equally between them. The act which they performed at music halls or when on exhibition was not a joint one, in that the husband could get work without the wife, but they were exceptionally dependent on each other, because they were midgets. When they were on tour they usually lived in a caravan parked near to their work in which they spent most of their time, as it was necessary that the public should not see them except at performances. The total period of the wife's incapacity for work was eight months after the accident, and during this period the husband, although himself fit and able to obtain work, chose to stay with her.

In an action by the plaintiffs for damages,

Ratio decidendi (the reasons given by the judge in favour of the plaintiffs) → **Held:** (i) the defendants were liable in damages for the following reasons—

(a) the defendants were under an absolute duty so to confine and control elephants kept by them that the elephants did no injury (dictum of LORD MACMILLAN in *Read* v. *J. Lyons & Co., Ltd.,* [1946] 2 All E.R. at p.476, applied), because elephants were a species that in law were within the class of dangerous animals, animals ferae naturae (*Filburn* v. *People's Palace & Aquarium Co., Ltd* (1890), 25 Q.B.D. 258, followed), and the injury had in fact been caused by the elephant while temporarily out of control);

(b) thus it was no defence either that the elephants concerned were not dangerous in fact, or that the injury or damage caused did not flow from any vicious act of the elephant, but was the result of the elephant's reaction to fright, or that the injury was caused by the

Appendix A: A Common Law Judgment 95

wrongful act of a stranger, viz., of W. (*Barker* v. *Snell,* [1909] 2 K.B. 825, explained and followed);

(c) nor did the maxim volenti non fit injuria afford a defence as the plaintiffs had no reason to suspect, when they engaged the booth, that elephants would come near, and when subsequently they knew that elephants would pass there was no obvious danger from them (*Clayards* v. *Dethick & Davis* (1848), 12 Q.B. 439 applied).

(ii) as regards damages—

(a) the total damages of both plaintiffs for loss of joint earnings for eight months should, in the circumstances, be apportioned equally between them, although the wife's part in the exhibition was less than her husband's;

(b) the husband was entitled only to one week's loss of his earnings for incapacity to earn due to ill health from nervous shock (*Owens* v. *Liverpool Corpn.,* [1938] 4 All E.R. 727, applied);

(c) although, therefore, the husband could not recover the half of the eight months' loss of joint earnings apportioned to him, yet he was entitled to damages for the period while he was fit to work and his wife was unfit, because his refusal to go on tour without his wife was, in the exceptional circumstances of the present case, reasonable and, if he had gone on tour, he would have been entitled to compensation for the cost of necessary domestic help and for the loss of his wife's society (*Burgess* v. *Florence Nightingale Hospital for Gentlewomen Management Committee,* [1955] 1 All E.R. 511, distinguished).

[As to liability for injuries by dangerous animals, see 1 HALSBURY'S LAWS (3rd Edn.) 666, para. 1272; and for cases on the subject, see 2 DIGEST 236-239, *238-244*.

As to the recovery of damages for nervous shock, see 11 HALSBURY'S LAWS (3rd Edn.) 278, para. 460; and for cases on the subject, see 17 DIGEST (Repl.) 122, 123, *333-339*, and 36 DIGEST (Repl.) 196, 197, *1032-1039*.]

References to textbooks where the law is discussed

Cases referred to:
(1) *Read* v. *Lyons (J.) & Co., Ltd.,* [1946] 2 All E.R. 471; [1947] A.C.156; [1947] L.J.R. 39; 175 L.T. 413; 36 Digest (Repl.) 83, 452.
(2) *M'Alister (or Donoghue)* v. *Stevenson,* [1932] A.C. 562; 1932 S.C. (H.L.) 31; 101 L.J.P.C. 119; 147 L.T. 281; 36 Digest (Repl.) 85, 458.

Previous decided cases for the guidance of the judge

96 Young People's Book of Law

(3) *Wormald* v. *Cole*, [1954] 1 All E.R. 683; [1954] 1 Q.B. 614; 3rd Digest Supp.
(4) *Filburn* v.*People's Palace & Aquarium Co., Ltd.,* (1890), 25 Q.B.D. 258; 59 L.J.Q.B. 471; 55 J.P. 181; 2 Digest 238, *243*.
(5) *McQuaker* v. *Goddard*, [1940] 1 All E.R. 471; [1940] 1 K.B. 687; 109 L.J.K.B. 673; 162 L.T. 232; 2nd Digest Supp.
(6) *Knott* v. *London County Council*, [1934] 1 K.B. 126; 103 L.J.K.B. 100; 150 L.T. 91; 97 J.P. 335; Digest Supp.
(7) *Parker* v. *Oloxo, Ltd & Senior*, [1937] 3 All E.R. 524; 36 Digest (Repl.) 87, *464*.
(8) *Glasgow Corpn.* v. *Muir*, [1943] 2 All E.R. 44; [1943] A.C. 448; 1943 S.C. (H.L.) 3; 112 L.J.P.C. 1; 169 L.T. 53; 107 J.P. 140; 36 Digest (Repl.) 58, 317.
(9) *Besozzi* v. *Harris*, (1858), 1 F. & F. 92; 175 E.R. 640; 2 Digest 238, *241*.
(10) *Clayards* v. *Dethick & Davis*, (1848), 12 Q.B. 439; 116 E.R. 932; 36 Digest (Repl.) 154, *809*.
(11) *Reardon Smith Line, Ltd.* v. *Australian Wheat Board*, [1956] 1 All E.R. 456; [1956] A.C. 266.
(12) *Baker* v. *Snell*, [1908] 2 K.B. 352; *affd.* C.A., [1908] 2 K.B. 825; 77 L.J.K.B. 1090; 99 L.T. 753; 2 Digest 240, *254*.
(13) *Rylands* v. *Fletcher*, (1868), L.R. 3 H.L. 330; 37 L.J.Ex. 161; 19 L.T. 220; 33 J.P. 70; 36 Digest (Repl.)282, *334*.
(14) *Hale* v. *Jennings Bros.,* [1938] 1 All E.R. 579; 36 Digest (Repl.) 286, *352*.
(15) *Owens* v. *Liverpool Corpn.*, [1938] 4 All E.R. 727; [1939] 1 K.B. 394: 108 L.J.K.B. 155; 160 L.T. 8; 17 Digest (Repl.) 123, *337*.
(16) *Burgess* v. *Florence Nightingale Hospital for Gentlewomen Management Committee*, [1955] 1 All E.R. 511; [1955] 1 Q.B. 349; 3rd Digest Supp.
(17) *Heath's Garage, Ltd.* v. *Hodges*, [1916] 2 K.B. 370; 85 L.J.K.B. 1289; 115 L.T. 129; 80 J.P. 321; 2 Digest 234, *226*.

Full description of the facts

Action

This was an action for damages by a husband and wife, Mr. and Mrs. J. H. W. Behrens, in respect of injuries which they sustained on Jan. 2, 1954, when a booth in which the plaintiffs were being exhibited in a fun fair adjoining a circus held by the defendants, Bertram Mills Circus, Ltd., was knocked down by one of the defendants' elephants with the result that the booth fell on Mrs.

Appendix A: A Common Law Judgment 97

Behrens (referred to hereinafter as the wife), causing her serious physical injuries, and, causing shock to Mr. Behrens (referred to hereinafter as the husband).

The defendants held a circus each year, and for this purpose they rented the Grand Hall at Olympia, London, and the annexe behind it. The main entrance to Olympia led into the Grand Hall. The circus ring and a theatre occupied that half of the hall nearer to the main entrance; the other half of the hall and the annexe contained the fun fair. Public access to the fun fair was obtained by the main entrance. A gallery ran round the Grand Hall, and the space underneath it, which was outside the theatre, formed a corridor, with small booths on either side of it which gave access to the main part of the fun fair. The passage-way between the booths was some thirteen feet wide and was primarily intended for the use of the public. The defendants operated the circus themselves, but not the fun fair. Although they retained general control of the fun fair, they granted concessions to different amusement caterers to set up various forms of entertainment there. At the further end of the annexe, beyond the fun fair, the defendants had a menagerie where they kept animals for show, including the animals who performed in the circus. Among these were six Burmese elephants. There were two performances of the circus on weekdays, and three on Saturdays, and at each performance the elephants were led from the menagerie to the circus ring and back again, on two separate occasions, once to take part in the grand parade round the circus ring, and, the second time, to perform their particular act. The route which the elephants took from the menagerie to the circus ring was along the passage-way between the booths.

The plaintiffs were dwarfs, or "midgets" as they were known in the amusement trade. The husband was only thirty inches high, and was uncommon in that he was perfectly proportioned; he claimed to be the smallest man on earth. The wife was thirty-six inches high and not perfectly proportioned. She was trained to play certain musical instruments with which she contributed to any act which the plaintiffs performed at music halls. Until 1949 the plaintiffs had appeared mainly in music halls, although they had also appeared with three circuses. In 1953 they went on tour with a Mr. Whitehead, who acted as their manager. On this tour they exhibited themselves in a booth, for admission to which a fee was charged to the public.

In August, 1953, the defendants granted to Mr. Whitehead a

licence to occupy a booth in the fun fair adjoining the defendants' circus at Olympia, for the purpose of exhibiting the plaintiffs Mr Whitehead paid the defendants £172 10s. for the licence, and the terms on which the plaintiffs and Mr. Whitehead worked were that the plaintiffs put up half the money required for the booth and took half the takings from it. They regarded themselves as partners with Mr. Whitehead, although in law, they were not partners. The booth occupied by the plaintiffs and Mr. Whitehead was in the corridor under the gallery on one side of the passage-way along which the elephants passed on their journeys between the menagerie and the circus ring. The booth had an exit and an entrance, between which was a paybox where Mr. Whitehead sat.

On the day of the accident, Jan. 2, 1954, Mr. Whitehead had arranged to get circus tickets for his two children, and to meet them, at 2 p.m. in the foyer of the main entrance to Olympia. The children duly arrived at the entrance together with a small Pomeranian dog called Simba, which belonged to Mr. Whitehead's daughter. Mr. Whitehead was unable to get circus tickets, and so he took the children to the fun fair and left them to wander around there. He then returned to the plaintiffs' booth with the dog Simba. Simba was put underneath the paybox counter in the booth, and its lead was attached to one of the legs of Mr. Whitehead's chair. The circus had already begun, and the elephants had made their first journey to and from the circus ring. They again came out of the menagerie to go to the circus ring to perform their act. They were walking in single file in their usual manner, with the trainer walking beside the leading elephant and a groom walking beside each of the remaining elephants. As the third elephant in the procession, called Bullu, was passing the plaintiffs' booth, the dog Simba ran out snapping and barking. Bullu trumpeted with fright, Simba turned back towards the booth, and Bullu went after her, followed by the elephant in front of Bullu. As a result, the front of the booth and other parts of it were knocked down and the wife, who was inside the booth with her husband, was seriously injured. The dog was killed. The trainer quickly got the elephants back into line, the whole incident having taken only a few seconds, and the elephants performed their act, as usual. Neither of the plaintiffs was touched by any of the elephants.

As a result of the accident the wife suffered the following injuries: fracture of the right arm, resulting in a shortening of the arm and restriction of its movement, fracture of five ribs (which healed well), a fracture of the lower part of the sacrum, and displacement of the coccyx. The last fracture united but caused her constant discomfort and pain. She came out of hospital on Mar. 10, 1954, and on June 12, 1954, she was examined by an orthopaedic surgeon, who then stated that she was fit to do light work which did not entail the skilled use of her arms. She was medically examined again in 1955, when it was stated that her general health had been detrimentally affected by the accident. She was again examined in 1956. At the time of this action, the wife was able to play musical instruments to the extent of providing supplementary interest while her husband was on stage, although she could not play as well as she had done before the accident. It was unnecessary to admit the husband to hospital after the accident, although he was very distressed on the day after the accident, and thereafter he went to bed for a week. As a further result of the accident, he suffered aggravation of an existing chest complaint.

The plaintiffs did not resume work until Apr. 1, 1956 (two and a quarter years after the accident), although in May or June, 1954, and at about the same time in 1955, they received offers of music hall work similar to that which they had previously done. The plaintiffs refused these offers, but it was not established that the plaintiffs rejected work for which they knew they were fit merely because they thought that acceptance might prejudice their claim for damages in this action.

Prior to the accident the plaintiffs were paid jointly at the rate of about £25 weekly; their expenses were, however, heavy and their net earnings were between £40 and £50 per month. Their takings and expenses in respect of their work were dealt with jointly and no part of the net earnings was appropriated as the special property of one or other of them. The act which the plaintiffs performed at music halls was not really a joint one; the husband was the main attraction as the supposedly smallest man on earth, and his perfect proportions were uncommon if not unique. His wife provided diversions of a musical kind, which could have been supplied in some other form, and her part in the act was subsidiary. Further, her musical act did not form part of the exhibition work which the plaintiffs were doing at Olympia and previously. The plaintiffs were, however, exceptionally dependent on each other because they were dwarfs. The husband was particularly dependent on his wife, and his dependence on her was increased by the fact that it was usual for them to live in a caravan which was parked near to their place of work and in which they had to spend most of their time, as he could not mingle with the public when he was being exhibited or was appearing in shows.

Names of the barristers in the case — *Harold Brown, Q.C., and F. B. Purchas* for the plaintiffs. *M. D. Van Oss* for the defendants.

Cur. adv. vult. ← The judge took time to decide

Name of the judge who decided the case: Mr Justice Devlin, one of Her Majesty's justices of the Queen's Bench

Jan. 30. DEVLIN, J., read a judgment in which he stated the facts which led up to and resulted in the accident which gave rise to the plaintiffs' claim, and continued: The plaintiffs rely on three causes of action, trespass, breach of the absolute duty laid on the keeper of a dangerous animal to confine and control it, and negligence. Counsel for the plaintiffs has not pursued before me the cause of action in trespass, while reserving his right to do so in a higher court.

The second cause of action, generally known as the scienter action, is the one on which counsel for the plaintiffs chiefly relied. Since one of the defendants' submissions goes to the root of that form of action, I propose to begin by stating just what I take its basis to be. Before doing this I must acknowledge my indebtedness to PROFESSOR GLANVILLE WILLIAMS, who in his book, LIABILITY FOR ANIMALS (1939), has dealt with the whole subject in such detail and with such clarity as to make it possible for me at least to hope that I can successfully grapple with this antiquated branch of the law and also to omit from this judgment much of the elaboration that would otherwise have to be there.

A person who keeps an animal with knowledge (scienter retinuit) of its tendency to do harm is strictly liable for damage that it does if it escapes; he is under an absolute duty to confine or control it so that it shall not do injury to others. All animals ferae naturae, that is, all animals which are not by nature harmless, such as a rabbit, or have not been tamed by man and domesticated such as a horse, are conclusively presumed to have such a tendency, so that the scienter need not in their case be proved. All animals in the second class, mansuetae naturae, are conclusively presumed to be harmless until they have manifested a savage or vicious propensity; proof of such a manifestation is proof of scienter and serves to transfer the animal, so to speak, out of its natural class into the class ferae naturae. In the book, LIABILITY FOR ANIMALS (1939), at p.265, PROFESSOR GLANVILLE WILLIAMS has traced the origin of "this primitive rule", as LORD MACMILLAN described it in *Read v. J. Lyons & Co., Ltd.* (1) ([1946] 2 All E.R. 471 at p. 476). No doubt, in its time it was a great improvement on the still more primitive notion that only the animal was "liable" for the harm which it did. But now this sort of doctrine with all its rigidity—its conclusive presumptions and categorisations—is outmoded and the law favours a flexible and circumstantial approach to problems of this sort. Four years ago, a committee appointed by the Lord Chancellor and presided over by LORD GODDARD, C.J., recommended that the scienter action should be abolished and that liability for harm done by an animal should be the same as in the case for any other chattel; it should depend on the failure to exercise the appropriate degree of care, which might in the case of very dangerous animals be "so stringent as to amount practically to a guarantee of safety":per LORD MACMILLAN in *M'Alister (or Donoghue)* v. *Stevenson* (2) ([1932] A.C. 562 at p.612). I wish to express the hope that Paliament may find time to consider this recommendation, for this branch of the law is badly in need of simplification.

The particular rigidity in the scienter action which is involved in this case—there are many others which are not—is the rule which requires the harmfulness of the offending animal to be judged, not by reference to its particular taming and habits, but by reference to the general habits of the species to which it belongs. The law ignores the world of difference between the wild elephant in the jungle and the trained elephant in the circus. The elephant Bullu is, in fact, no more dangerous than a cow; she reacted in the same way as a cow would do to the irritation of a small dog; if perhaps her bulk made her capable of doing more damage, her higher training enabled her to be more swiftly checked. I am, however, compelled to assess the defendants' liability in this case in just the same way as I would assess it if they had loosed a wild elephant into the fun fair. This is a branch of the law which, as LORD GODDARD, C.J. (quoting BLACKBURN, J.) said recently in *Wormald* v. *Cole* (3) ([1954] 1 All E.R. 683 at p. 686), has been settled by authority rather than by reason. But once the fundamental irrationality is accepted of treating circus elephants as if they were wild, I think is is possible to determine sensibly in the light of the scienter rule the other points on liability which arise in this case.

The defendants submit five answers to the scienter action. They are: (i) that the elephants are not ferae naturae within the meaning of the rule; (ii) that the rule does not impose liability for every act that an animal does if it escapes control, but only for those acts which are vicious and savage, which the action of Bullu was not; (iii) that the plaintiffs' injuries were caused by their own fault; (iv) that the maxim volenti non fit injuria— that is, that the plaintiffs accepted the risk— applies to them; (v) that it is a good defence to liabilty under the rule if the action of the animal is caused by the wronful act of a third party, in this case Mr. Whitehead and the dog Simba.

The first submission is, in my judgment, concluded so far as this court is concerned, by the decision of the Court of Appeal in *Filburn* v. *People's Palace & Aquarium Co., Ltd.* (4) ([1890], 25 Q.B.D. 258), which held that, as a matter of law, an elephant is an animal ferae naturae. Counsel for the defendants sought to distinguish this case on the ground that the elephants belonging to the defendants are Burmese elephants and he submits that it is open to me to hold that, while elephants generally are ferae naturae, Burmese elephants are not. In my judgment, it is not open to me to consider this submission. It is not stated in *Filburn* v. *People's Palace & Aquarium Co., Ltd.* (4) what the nationality of the elephant was with which the court was there dealing, and the case must be regarded as an authority for the legal position that all elephants are dangerous. The reason why this is a question of law and not question of fact is because it is a matter of which judicial notice has to be taken. The doctrine has, from its foundation, proceeded on the supposition that the knowledge of what kinds of animals are tame and what are savage is common knowledge. Evidence is receivable, if at all, only on the basis that the judge may wish to inform himself. This was clearly settled by the Court of Appeal in *McQuaker* v. *Goddard* (5) ([1940] 1 All E.R., where CLAUSON L.J., said (ibid., at p. 478):

"The reason why the evidence was given was so that it might assist the judge in forming his view as to what the ordinary course of nature in this regard in fact is, a matter of which he is supposed to have complete knowledge."

Common knowledge about the ordinary course of nature will extend to a knowledge of the propensities of animals according to their different genera, but cannot be supposed to extend to the manner of behaviour of animals of the same genus in different parts of the world. Nor can one begin a process of inquiry which might lead in many directions (for example, I am told that female elephants are more docile than male, and that that is why circus elephants are usually female) and be productive of minute subdivisions which would destroy the generality of the rule.

The defendants' second contention raises a point of doubt and difficulty. It may be approached in this way. The reason for imposing

Appendix A: A Common Law Judgment 103

a specially stringent degree of liability on the keeper of a savage animal is that such an animal has a propensity to attack mankind and, if left unrestrained, would be likely to do so. The keeper has, therefore, in the words of LORD MACMILLAN in *Read* v. *J. Lyons & Co., Ltd.* (1) ([1946] 2 All E.R. 471 at p. 476), "an absolute duty to confine or control it so that it shall not do injury . . .". If, however, it escapes from his control, is he liable (subject, of course, to the rules on remoteness of damage) for any injury which it causes, or only for such injury as flows naturally from its vicious or savage propensity? Counsel for the defendants submits that it is the latter part of this question which suggests the correct answers and that the rule of absolute liability applies only when an animal is acting savagely and attacking human beings. On the facts of this case, he submits that Bullu was acting, not viciously, but out of fright; she was seeking to drive off the small dog rather than attack it; it may be that she or another elephant trampled on the dog (there is no conclusive evidence of that, and it might have been crushed by falling timber) but there is nothing to show that she trampled on it deliberately. Certainly she never attacked the wife, who was injured only indirectly. In short, if Bullu could be treated as a human being, her conduct would be described, not as vicious, but as quite excusable.

It does not, to my mind, necessarily follow that the scope of the rule is co-extensive with the reason for making it. It may equally well be argued that, once the rule is made, the reason for making it is dissolved and all that then matters are the terms of the rule. That would certainly be the right approach in the case of any statutory rule of absolute liability. Is it so in the case of this rule of common law? There appears to be no authority directly in point. Counsel for the defendants derives the chief support for his contention from an argument which may be summarised as follows. If an animal mansuetae naturae manifests a vicious tendency, the scienter rule applies to it as if it were ferae naturae. The law has often been put in that way, for example, by LORD WRIGHT, in *Knott* v. *London County Council* (6) ([1934] 1 K.B. 126 at p. 139). How is the principle applied? Suppose that a large dog collides with a child and knocks him down, that is an accident and not a manifestation of a vicious propensity and the scienter rule does not apply at all: if the dog bites a child, it becomes ferae naturae and the strict rule thereafter applies. It would, however, seem to be unreasonable that the strict rule should require the dog to be kept under complete restraint. Suppose that its keeper muzzles it and that while muzzled the dog playfully or accidently knocks a child down, ought tne keeper to be liable? There is a good deal of authority referred to by PROFESSOR GLANVILLE WILLIAMS, to show that the keeper is not liable; and the learned author considers that the damage must have in some way been intended by the animal, that its benevolence or its mens rea is relevant and that, at least in the case of harmless animals, the rule is that the injury must be the result of a vicious propensity.

This is an impressive argument. It does not seem to me, however, that the logic of the matter necessarily requires that an animal which is savage by disposition should be put on exactly the same footing as one which is savage by nature. Certainly, practical considerations would seem to demand that they should be treated differently. It may be unreasonable to hold the owner of a biting dog responsible thereafter for everything that it does; but it may also be unreasonable to admit the liability for a tiger. If a person wakes up in the middle of the night and find an escaping tiger on top of his bed and suffers a heart attack, it would be nothing to the point that the intentions of the tiger were quite amiable. If a tiger is let loose in a fun fair, it seems to me to be irrelevant whether a person is injured as a result of a direct attack, or because, on seeing it, he runs away and falls over. The feature of this present case which is constantly arising to blur the reasoning is that fact that this particular elephant, Bullu, was tame; but that, as I have said, is a fact which must be ignored. She is to be treated as if she were a wild elephant, and, if a wild elephant were let loose in the fun fair and were stampeding around, I do not think that there would be much difficulty in holding that a person who was injured by falling timber had a right to redress. It is not, in my judgment, practicable to introduce conceptions of mens rea and malevolence in the case of animals.

The distinction between those animals which are ferae naturae by virtue of their genus and those which become so by the exhibition of a paricular habit seems to me to be this: that in the case of the former it is assumed (and the assumption is true of a really dangerous animal such as a tiger) that whenever they get out of control they are practically bound to do injury, while in the case of the latter the assumption is that they will do injury only to the extent of the propensity which they have peculiarly manifested. It would not be at all irrational if the law were to recognise a limited distinction of this sort while holding that both classes of animals are governed by the same scienter rule. In the case of dangerous chattels, for example, the law has recognised, although it is not perhaps now of much importance, the distinction between chattels that are dangerous in themselves and chattels that are dangerous when used for certain purposes; and animals ferae naturae have frequently been compared with chattels in the former class; see, for example, per HILBERY, J., in *Parker v. Oloxo, Ltd. & Senior* (7) ([1937] 3 All E.R. 524 at p.528), and per LORD WRIGHT in *Glasgow Corpn. v. Muir* (8) ([1943] 2 All E.R. 44 at p. 52).

As I have said, there is really no authority on this point. There are, indeed, not many cases which have dealt with an animal that is ferae naturae by genus as distinct from disposition. In such cases as there are—*Besozzi v. Harris* (9) ((1858), 1 F.& F. 92) and *Filburn v. People's Palace & Aquarium Co., Ltd.* (4)—the rule was stated in the widest terms, but in these cases the court was dealing with an attacking animal, so that the point did not arise. Nevertheless, in my judgement, they laid down the principle which I should follow: and I think that the statement of the law by LORD MACMILLAN, in *Read v. J. Lyons & Co., Ltd.* (1) ([1949] 2 All E.R. 471 at p. 476) which I have quoted, namely, that there is "an absolute duty to confine or control [a dangerous animal] so that it shall not do injury" needs no qualification.

This conclusion is supported by *Wormald v. Cole* (3). I do not rely on that decision as an authority which is directly in point because it concerned the rule of absolute liability for cattle trespass, and these rules of absolute liability, while similar in effect, have different origins; but it furnishes strong support by way of analogy. In that case the plaintiff, when she was trying to get straying cattle out of her garden, was injured, not because they had attacked her, but because in blundering about they had knocked her down. It was argued that the plaintiff could not recover because her injuries were not the result of any vicious action on the part of the cattle. This argument was rejected by the Court of Appeal. LORD GODDARD, C.J., pointed out ([1954] 1 All E.R. at p.688) that in many cases it would be impossible to say with certainty whether the injuries were caused by vice, or playfulness, or by mere accident.

It follows that, subject to any special defence, the defendants are liable for any injury done while the elephant was out of control. It does not follow (I say this because of a point that was raised in the argument) that if an elephant slips and stumbles, its keeper is responsible for the consequences. There must be a failure of control. Here, however, there was such a failure, albeit a very temporary one. It follows also that the ordinary rule on remoteness of damage applies. It was not suggested that, if an animal which is out of control knocks over a structure and injures a person the other side of it, that is not, under the ordinary rule, a consequence of the failure of control.

The third point taken by the defendants is that the injuries were due to the plaintiffs' own fault. This defence is of a nature well recognised in this class of case and there are many cases in which liability has been successfully contested on the ground that the savage animal was teased or provoked by the plaintiff. I see no reason why the same sort of defence should not prevail where the fault of the plaintiff does not amount to recklessness of this sort, but is failure of due diligence to look after his own safety. The facts said to constitute the defence in this case are pleaded in para. 6A of the re-amended defence:

> "Further or in the alternative the matters complained of were caused or contributed to by the negligence of the plaintiffs and each of them in that they permitted the said dog to be in or near to the said booth well knowing that dogs were not permitted upon the circus premises and/or that dogs were likely to alarm or excite the elephants."

In my judgment, this plea breaks down completely on the allegation that the plaintiffs permitted the dog to be in or near the booth. Even if I were to assume that the plaintiffs knew of the presence of the dog and to assume likewise the other allegations in the paragraph, there is nothing at all to sustain the allegation of permission. Mr. Whitehead was not in their employ and they had no power to control him in any way. Conceivably, it might be said that, if the presence of the dog amounted to an obvious danger, anyone who knew of it, whether he had the power to order the dog off or not, ought in the interests of his own safety to have reported it to someone who had the necessary authority; but no one puts the danger as high as that.

The fourth contention of the defendants is a plea of volenti non fit injuria, based on the allegation that the plaintiffs accepted any risk inherent in the passage of the elephants past their booth. There is no evidence that either the plaintiffs or Mr. Whitehead knew or had any reason to suspect when the licence was granted that the elephants would come anywhere near their booth. Counsel for the defendant, however, submits that the time when the licence was entered into is not the decisive time, or not the only decisive time. He submits that, when the plaintiffs discovered, as of course they did at the beginning, that the elephants passed the booth, their decision to remain amounted to an assumption of the risk. The situation at this later point of time raises quite different considerations. The plaintiffs had then to decide, in the light of their knowledge of the conditions under which it would have to be exercised, not whether they would acquire a right, but whether they would continue to exercise a right for which they had already paid. It is not per se a defence that the plaintiffs were engaged in exercising a right. The pursuit of one's own rights may sometimes be so foolhardy that the reasonable man should desist and seek another remedy. If a man is on the highway and he sees elephants approaching in procession, the law does not require him to elect between turning down a side street or accepting the risk of their misbehaviour if he goes on: but if he sees them stampeding and remains where he is because he considers that he has as much right to the highway as they have, he might fail to recover. I take the law on this point as that laid down in *Clayards* v. *Dethick & Davis* (10) ((1848), 12 Q.B. 439). In that case the defendants made an open trench outside the plaintiff's stable and told him he must put up with it. The plaintiff attempted to get his horse out by means of planks over the trench and was advised by the defendants not to do so because it was dangerous. An accident occurred and the plaintiff was held entitled to recover. He was not bound to refrain from exercising his rights because there was some danger. As PATTERSON J., put it (ibid., at p. 446):

> "The whole question was, whether the danger was so obvious that the plaintiff could not with common prudence make the attempt."

The same principle has recently been considered in the Privy Council in *Reardon Smith Line, Ltd.* v. *Australian Wheat Board* (11) ([1956] 1 All E.R. 456 at p. 461). It cannot here be contended that the passing of the elephants created an obvious danger; indeed, the case as pleaded by the defendants is that the risk was very small. This plea fails.

The last of the defendants' contentions is that they are freed from liability by the wrongful act of a third party. This point appears to be concluded against them by the decision of the Court of Appeal in *Baker* v. *Snell* (12) ([1908] 2 K.B. 825), in which it was held by a majority that the intervening act of a third party was no defence. But counsel for the plaintiffs, perhaps because he had his eye on the place where *Baker* v. *Snell* (12) would naught avail him, or perhaps because he feared that I might be deterred from following the decision by the volume of criticism that has since flowed over it, gave it no place in the van of his argument—non tali auxilio, except, of course, in the alternative. He preferred to rely on general principles, rather than on any specific authority, for his chief submission on this point. He submitted that the liability in respect of a savage animal was based on the rule in *Rylands* v. *Fletcher* (13) ((1868), L.R. 3 H.L. 330). That rule allows as a defence the act of a third party only if it is the act of a stranger; and a licensee is not, he submitted, to be regarded as a stranger. Mr. Whitehead was a licensee and, therefore, his intervention afforded no excuse.

There are in the authorities numerous dicta to suggest that the liability for savage animals is a branch of the rule in *Rylands* v. *Fletcher* (13). In his book LIABILITY FOR ANIMALS (1939), at p. 352, note 4, PROFESSOR GLANVILLE WILLIAMS has collected the cases. These dicta may have to be reconsidered in the light of what was said in *Read* v. *J. Lyons & Co., Ltd.* (1) ([1946] 2 All E.R. 471), particularly per VISCOUNT SIMON (ibid., at p. 474). Whether or not the two rules stem from a common principle, it would, no doubt, be legitimate in formulating the exception, if any, to the liability, for savage animals to look at exceptions that have already been established under other rules of strict liability. But, whether the process be one of analogy or one of derivation, it must be remembered that the underlying conditions for the two kinds of liability are different. One is based on the possession of an animal and the other on the occupation of land. If, in relation to the former, the holding of a licence is to have any materiality, it must refer to some licensed custodian of the animal, such as the potman in *Baker* v. *Snell* (12). The fact that in this particular case the defendants not only were the keepers of the elephant but had also rented the premises on which the animal was at the time of the accident and licensed the third party to be on them is wholly irrelevant to any question of liability in the scienter action. If the defendants had granted a concession for the performance of the circus or the keeping of a menagerie as well as for the fun fair, and, accordingly, the elephant had been kept by some other defendant, it could not possibly be relevant in an action against him to show that the defendant and a third party were both concessionaires or licensees of the same licensor. It cannot make any difference in principle if the keeper of the animal happens also to be the licensor. In my judgment, therefore, if the rule in *Rylands* v. *Fletcher* (13) is to be applied, Mr. Whitehead must be deemed for its purposes to be a stranger.

Counsel for the plaintiffs relied on *Hale* v. *Jennings Bros*. (14) ([1938] 1 All E.R. 579), particularly the observations of SLESSER, L.J., at p. 583. If in this case I were dealing with liability which arose out of the occupation of land, these dicta would be in point. For the reasons which I have given, I think that they are irrelevant in determining the status of Mr. Whitehead. I do not mean that the relationship of licensor and licensee is necessarily irrelevant on consequential issues of fact. Accepting Mr. Whitehead as a stranger, it would still be necessary for the defendants to show that they took all reasonable precautions to prevent him or any other stranger from interfering with their animals; and it might well be that reasonable precautions would include, since they happened incidentally to be licensors, using their powers under the licence to control his conduct, for example by forbidding dogs. That, however, would raise another point which would go to an issue of negligence. That is an answer to the third party defence which could arise on the facts and in that light I shall refer to it again, but, in my judgment, Mr. Whitehead's status as a licensee does not of itself dispose of that defence as a matter of law.

I turn to *Baker* v. *Snell* (12). In that case the defendant was a publican who owned a dog known by him to be savage. It was the duty of his potman to let the dog out early in the morning and then chain it up again. On the occasion in question the potman brought the dog into the kitchen where the plaintiff, who was a housemaid in the employment of the defendant, was at breakfast and saying: "I will bet the dog will not bite anyone in the room", let it go saying: "Go it, Bob". The dog then flew at the plaintiff and bit her. In the county court the judge held that the act of the potman was an assault for which the defendant was not liable and he non-suited the plaintiff. The non-suit was attacked on two grounds. It was contended that the defendant was liable as the keeper of the dog and that the intervening act of the potman, even if he had been a stranger, would be no defence. Secondly, it was contended that, if the intervention did provide a good ground for defence, nevertheless, since in this case the intervener was the defendant's servant and acting within the scope of his employment, the defendant must be liable on that ground. A new trial was ordered both in the Divisional Court ([1908]

2 K.B. 352) and on appeal by the Court of Appeal and in both courts the judges were unanimous; but they were not unanimous in their reasons. In the Court of Appeal, all three of the lords justices agreed that the question whether or not the potman was acting in the course of his employment was one of fact which ought to have been left to the jury and that a new trial must be ordered on that score. COZENS-HARDY, M.R., and FARWELL, L.J., considered also, as had SUTTON, J., in the court below ([1908] 2 K.B. 352 at p. 355), that the defendant was liable as the keeper of the animal and that the intervention of the potman, even if not acting in the course of his employment, created no defence. Even on this view a new trial was necessary as it was not open to the Court of Appeal to assess the damages. On this point KENNEDY, L.J., disagreed, sharing the view expressed by CHANNELL, J., in the Divisional Court.

It is not, I think, disputed that, if the reasoning of COZENS-HARDY, M.R., and FARWELL, L. J., is binding on me, I must dismiss without further inquiry a defence based on the act of Mr. Whitehead. Counsel for the defendants submits that the gist of the decision was the order for a new trial on the grounds on which the lords justices were unanimous and that the observations of the Master of the Rolls and FARWELL, L. J., on the other point should be treated as obiter. This question depends, I think, on the language used by COZENS-HARDY, M. R. It is well established that, if a judge gives two reasons for his decision, both are binding. It is not permissible to pick out one as being supposedly the better reason and ignore the other one; nor does it matter for this purpose which comes first and which comes second. The practice of making judicial observations obiter is also well established. A judge may often give additional reasons for his decision without wishing to make them part of the ratio decidendi; he may not be sufficiently convinced of their cogency as to want them to have the full authority of precedent, and yet may wish to state them so that those who later may have the duty of investigating the same point will start with some guidance. This is a matter which the judge himself is alone capable of deciding and any judge who comes after him must ascertain which course has been adopted from the language used and not by consulting his own preference.

COZENS-HARDY, M. R., first dealt with the judgment of CHANNELL, J., and agreed his view that the scope of the potman's employment ought to have been left to the jury. He said ([1908] 2 K.B. at p.828):

Obiter dicta
(Observations by the judge not strictly necessary to his decision)

Appendix A: A Common Law Judgment   111

> "I entirely adopt that view, and that, no doubt, is in itself a sufficient reason for affirming the decision of the court below, but as a matter of wider interest has been raised, and as it has been dealt with by both CHANNELL and SUTTON, J. J., I think it right to state, shortly, my view on the point."

If this passage had stood by itself, I think that I should have probably construed it as signifying that the Master of the Rolls did not wish— as would be quite natural in a case where there was a considerable conflict of judicial opinion— to give the force of precedent to views which were not necessary to the decision in the case. But after he had considered the other point and expressed his view about it, he said this (ibid., at p. 832):

> "On these authorities, and in accordance with what in my judgment is settled law, I think that the matter ought to go down for a new trial, not merely on the ground stated by CHANNELL, J., though I agree that is sufficient, but also on the ground as to which he expressed some doubt, but on which SUTTON, J., appears to have based his decision."

In this final sentence of his judgment I think that COZENS-HARDY, M.R., was clearly basing his decision on the two grounds and that it is not open to me to choose between them. I have said that this point depends on the language of COZENS-HARDY, M. R., because I think that it is plain from the language used by FARWELL, L. J., that he gave as the principal ground for his judgement that the wrongful act of a third person was no defence.

Accordingly, I hold this contention, viz., that the wrongful act of a third party is a good defence to liability under the scienter rule, which is the last of the defendants' contentions, to be concluded against the defendants by authority which binds me. The result is, therefore, that the rule of strict liability applies and the defendants must compensate the plaintiffs for their injuries.

I have reached this conclusion on the law without having to go very deeply into the facts, and indeed, on the basis of facts which were almost all undisputed. There was, however, a good deal of dispute on other questions of fact which may become relevant if different conclusions are reached on the law. I shall, by way of any appendix to this judgment, set out my findings on these points in case they may be material hereafter; but before I do that I must deal with the assessment of damages which also raises some difficult questions of fact and law.

[HIS LORDSHIP described the injuries suffered by the wife, and continued:] The item in the claim for damages which gives rise to most difficulty, both on the facts and on the law, is the claim for loss of earnings. I cannot, however, give joint damages and it will be necessary for me to consider how far each of the plaintiffs individually has suffered a financial loss as the result of his or her injuries respectively. It will also be necessary for me to consider whether the husband is entitled in law to recover for financial loss caused to him as a result of the injuries which his wife sustained. Before I do this I think it would be convenient, in order to get at the true facts about the loss of earnings, to put these matters momentarily on one side and consider how far the accident affected their joint earning power.

[HIS LORDSHIP considered the facts and, after saying that he accepted the submission of counsel for the defendants that the plaintiffs' act was not a joint act and that diversions other than those provided by the wife could have been arranged for the husband's act, continued:] I am also satisfied, however, that it would not be reasonable to expect the husband to go touring or to go round fairgrounds and exhibitions by himself and without the company of his wife. The plaintiffs live in a strange world and the bond between them must be much stronger even that the ordinary tie of matrimony. [After referring to medical examinations of the wife in 1955, HIS LORDSHIP said that, beyond a statement made in the medical report in 1955, which was not repeated in the report of 1956, that her general health was detrimentally affected, there was nothing to show to what extent, if at all, she was unfit to accompany her husband on his tours. HIS LORDSHIP continued:] I think that the discomfort which the wife has while sitting and possibly some deterioration in her general health might make the help which she can give to her husband in his professional life more arduous that it would otherwise have been, and that this is a proper consideration in estimating the appropriate figure for her general damages; but I am satisfied that there is no evidence on which I could find that her incapacity lasted until Apr. 1, 1956, the date on which the plaintiffs first commenced work after the accident.

There is one remaining factor in the plaintiffs' joint earning power to be considered. Even if the case for the joint act had been fully made out and even if I had held that the husband's career on the stage was finished, it would still have been open to him to earn his living by exhibition at fun fairs and the like as he was doing at Olympia at the time of the accident. I am satisfied that while exhibition work might not be so congenial to the husband and while his having to resort to it more extensively in the future than in the past might be an element (if legally relevant) to be taken into account in assessing general damages, no case has, in any event, been made out for the contention that the wife's injuries put an end to his professional livelihood. For these reasons I am satisfied that no diminution in joint earning power has been proved after the time when the wife was up and about again and fit to accompany her husband on his travels. Any liability on the defendants for loss of earnings must, therefore, come to an end as soon as she was fit to accompany her husband. Treating them as joint earners, they could then have got work at the pre-accident remuneration. In the face of the evidence that the wife was fit for light work in the middle of June 1954, and in the absence of any evidence that she was unfit to go with her husband on tour, I find it impossible to say that the defendants' liability for loss of earnings can extend much beyond that date. I think that the plaintiffs were entitled to some period after recovery to look around for work; but if I fix the total period of incapacity at eight months, I think that that is as much as I can do. I assess the joint loss of earnings for that period at £360.

I must now proceed to consider what proportion this special damage is recoverable as between the two plaintiffs, and whether the husband has a good cause of action in respect of the whole of his proportion, and what sums should be awarded to each plaintiff individually as general damages.

I shall take the wife first. She received half the benefit of the joint earnings and may, therefore, be taken to have been paid half. It is, in my judgment, nothing to the point to submit that, as her part of the act was much smaller than that of her husband, she was, commercially speaking, worth less than half. So long as the arrangement was a genuine one and husband and wife, rightly or wrongly regarded their contributions as being of equal value, the loss to the wife is a loss of what she was getting and not of what she would have got if her husband had been disposed to drive a harder bargain. This approach to the subject affects the wife's general damage as well as her special, and in the case of the general damage it works for the advantage of the defendants. I am satisfied that in the future as in the past her husband will continue to rate the support that he gets from the wife as being worth half the joint earnings; therefore, so long as he is alive and working her disablement will not cause her any professional loss. I think that her damages, both special and general, must be assessed on this basis. Accordigly, I award £180 as special damages to the wife.

The wife's general damages must be substantial. Her injuries were considerable and they have left some permanent effects of pain and discomfort, I have to take into account that the discomfort, if not pain, which her injuries continue to cause her may well make her work with her husband more arduous and I have to assess her damages in the light of the arduous work which she had to do if by her support of her husband she is to earn her share of the joint takings. I have also to consider that her ability to earn her own living, if her husband should die, had been diminished by her inability to perform a musical act on her own. I assess her general damages at £2,750.

I turn now to the husband's claim. Can he be compensated for the loss of half the joint earnings? That raises one question of law and another is raised in the assessment of the general damages. I shall take the latter first. The real claim presented by counsel for the plaintiffs is for fright. The elephant coming over the top of a booth would be a terrifying thing even for an ordinary man, and, although the husband asserts that he was not frightened, I am satisfied that the shock must have been considerable. I should like to award him a substantial sum under this head but I am satisfied that I cannot do so except to the extremely limited extent that the shock resulted in physical or mental harm. I think that that is clearly the effect of the authorities. When the word "shock" is used in them, it is not in the sense of a mental reaction but in a medical sense as the equivalent of nervous shock: MACKINNON, L.J., in *Owens* v. *Liverpool Corpn.* (15) ([1938] 4 All E.R. 717), refers to it (ibid., at p. 730) as being "ascertainable by the physician" and (ibid., at p. 731) as "the form of ill health known as shock". I appreciate that it is now becoming increasingly difficult to define the boundaries of mental ill health. Without infringing the general principle embedded in the common law that mental suffering caused by grief, fear, anguish and the like is not assessable, *Owens* v. *Liverpool Corpn.* (15) goes as far as any court can go and I cannot accept the invitation of counsel for the plaintiffs to attempt an extension of what is there said.

[HIS LORDSHIP referred to the husband's medical history after the accident and to the fact that the husband went to bed on the day after the accident and remained there for a week, and continued:] I think it would not be unreasonable if I were to treat that, namely, the week in bed, as some form of nervous prostration which amounted to ill health. The husband was thus unable to earn money during that period, although that would probably have been impossible anyway owing to the destruction of the booth; the defendants were not, however, concerned to explore this minutely. I assess the damages under this head at £25. [HIS LORDSHIP referred to the evidence that the shock suffered by the husband had had a detrimental effect on an existing chest complaint, and said;] I should have thought it likely that, in the case of a man over sixty years of age, minor chest troubles might begin, in any event, to get slightly worse. Here again, however, the defendants have not been disposed to niggle, and I assess the damages under this head at £50. Apart from loss of earnings, the items of special damage particularised in the statement of claim have been agreed to amount to £235, and the defendants are willing to accept that these items are all properly chargeable by the husband without going into their responsibility for them in law.

There is, therefore, left only the husband's claim for loss of half the joint earnings. I take £10 of this loss as being included in the figure of £25 which I have already awarded in respect of his own physical incapacity. The balance of £170 depends on whether he is entitled to compensation in respect of the period when he was fit to work and his wife was not. If the husband's loss consisted simply of the fact that the loss of his wife's musical talent made the joint act less valuable to him, I should hold that he could not recover. I decided that way in *Burgess* v. *Florence Nightingale Hospital for Gentlewomen Management Committee* (16) ([1955] 1 All E.R. 511), where a similar point arose under the Fatal Accidents Act, 1846. But that is not the point here. I have found as a fact that the husband has proved no loss under that head. His loss lies in the fact that his wife would, if he had gone on tour, have been unable to give him the society and domestic help which only she as a wife could give. In *Burgess* v. *Florence Nightingale Hospital for Gentlewomen Management Committee* (16) it was not suggested that the arrangement between the parties in that case depended in any way on the relationship of husband and wife.

If the husband during his wife's incapacity had gone on tour, he might have had to have paid someone to take her place on the stage and he would also have had to have paid someone to look after him in the caravan. The first payment he could not have recovered from the defendants; on the facts he would have sustained no loss, since he would not have had to have paid his wife her share of the earnings and she would have her own independent claim for the loss of that share; in law the loss, if he had sustained it, would not be recoverable. But the second payment he could have recovered, and, I think, have added to it a claim for compensation for the loss of his wife's society which no substitute domestic help could give. If she could not be with him in her customary place, it would not, to my mind, matter that that place was a caravan and not the ordinary matrimonial home. It would not be merely an impairment of the consortium, but a total, though temporary, loss of it. In fact, however, he did not go on tour. He preferred to stay at home and accept the loss of earnings; and in the very peculiar circumstances of this case I have held that his choice was a reasonable one. Can he then recover his loss of earnings as damages? To hold that he can may be breaking new ground in this type of action, but I can see no reason in principle why he should not be thus compensated. The assessment of damages must be governed by those principles which apply generally in the law of tort and, provided he acts reasonably, he must be put in as good a position, so far as money can do it, as if the wrong had not been done to him. I repeat that on the facts this is a most exceptional case, turning on the exceptional need which the husband had for the support of his wife as a wife. Because of that I think that he is entitled to recover. The result is that there will be judgment for the husband for sums totalling £480, and for the wife for £2,930.

[HIS LORDSHIP then considered further issues of fact which were not necessary for his judgment in view of his decision on the law but which might become necessary in the event of a different view of the law being taken by an appellate court.]

Judgment for the plaintiff husband for £480 and for the plaintiff wife for £2,930.

Solicitors: *Charlton Hubbard & Co.,* agents for *Marsh & Ferriman,* Worthing (for the plaintiffs); *William Charles Crocker* (for the defendants).

[*Reported by* WENDY SHOCKETT, Barrister-at-Law].

Appendix B: Example of a Statute

Royal Coat of Arms

Animals Act 1971

Title of Act

CHAPTER 22

Place where Found when all Acts of 1971 are printed together

ARRANGEMENT OF SECTIONS

Strict liability for damage done by animals

Section
1. New provisions as to strict liability for damage done by animals.
2. Liability for damage done by dangerous animals.
3. Liability for injury done by dogs to livestock.
4. Liability for damage and expenses due to trespassing livestock.
5. Exceptions from liability under sections 2 to 4.
6. Interpretation of certain expressions used in sections 2 to 5.

Detention and sale of trespassing livestock

7. Detention and sale of trespassing livestock.

Animals straying on to highway

8. Duty to take care to prevent damage from animals straying on to the highway.

Protection of livestock against dogs

9. Killing of or injury to dogs worrying livestock.

Supplemental

10. Application of certain enactments to liability under sections 2 to 4.
11. General interpretation.
12. Application to Crown.
13. Short title, repeal, commencement and extent.

Animals Act 1971 c. 22

ELIZABETH II

1971 CHAPTER 22

An Act to make provision with respect to civil liability for damage done by animals and with respect to the protection of livestock from dogs; and for purposes connected with those matters. [12th May 1971] ← Preamble

← Date when Royal Assent given

BE IT ENACTED by the Queen's most Excellent Majesty, by and with the advice and consent of the Lords Spiritual and Temporal, and Commons, in this present Parliament assembled, and by the authority of the same, as follows:— ← Enacting Formula (going back to 15th century)

Strict liability for damage done by animals

Number of section → 1.—(1) The provisions of sections 2 to 5 of this Act replace—

(a) the rules of the common law imposing a strict liability in tort for damage done by an animal on the ground that the animal is regarded as ferae naturae or that its vicious or mischievous propensities are known or presumed to be known;

(b) subsections (1) and (2) of section 1 of the Dogs Act 1906 as amended by the Dogs (Amendment) Act 1928 (injury to cattle or poultry); and

(c) the rules of the common law imposing a liability for cattle trespass.

New provisions as to strict liability for damage done by animals.

1906 c. 32.
1928 c. 21.

Number of sub-section → (2) Expressions used in those sections shall be interpreted in accordance with the provisions of section 6 (as well as those of section 11) of this Act.

Side notes telling you what the section is about ↓

2.—(1) Where any damage is caused by an animal which belongs to a dangerous species, any person who is a keeper of the animal is liable for the damage, except as otherwise provided by this Act.

Liability for damage done by dangerous animals.

(2) Where damage is caused by an animal which does not belong to a dangerous species, a keeper of the animal is liable for the damage, except as otherwise provided by this Act, if—
- (a) the damage is of a kind which the animal, unless restrained, was likely to cause or which, if caused by the animal, was likely to be severe ; and
- (b) the likelihood of the damage or of its being severe was due to characteristics of the animal which are not normally found in animals of the same species or are not normally so found except at particular times or in particular circumstances ; and
- (c) those characteristics were known to that keeper or were at any time known to a person who at that time had charge of the animal as that keeper's servant or, where that keeper is the head of a household, were known to another keeper of the animal who is a member of that household and under the age of sixteen.

Liability for injury done by dogs to livestock.

3. Where a dog causes damage by killing or injuring livestock, any person who is a keeper of the dog is liable for the damage, except as otherwise provided by this Act.

Liability for damage and expenses due to trespassing livestock.

4.—(1) Where livestock belonging to any person strays on to land in the ownership or occupation of another and—
- (a) damage is done by the livestock to the land or to any property on it which is in the ownership or possession of the other person ; or
- (b) any expenses are reasonably incurred by that other person in keeping the livestock while it cannot be restored to the person to whom it belongs or while it is detained in pursuance of section 7 of this Act, or in ascertaining to whom it belongs ;

the person to whom the livestock belongs is liable for the damage or expenses, except as otherwise provided by this Act.

(2) For the purposes of this section any livestock belongs to the person in whose possession it is.

Exceptions from liability under sections 2 to 4.

5.—(1) A person is not liable under sections 2 to 4 of this Act for any damage which is due wholly to the fault of the person suffering it.

(2) A person is not liable under section 2 of this Act for any damage suffered by a person who has voluntarily accepted the risk thereof.

(3) A person is not liable under section 2 of this Act for any damage caused by an animal kept on any premises or structure to a person trespassing there, if it is proved either—
- (a) that the animal was not kept there for the protection of persons or property ; or

(b) (if the animal was kept there for the protection of persons or property) that keeping it there for that purpose was not unreasonable.

(4) A person is not liable under section 3 of this Act if the livestock was killed or injured on land on to which it had strayed and either the dog belonged to the occupier or its presence on the land was authorised by the occupier.

(5) A person is not liable under section 4 of this Act where the livestock strayed from a highway and its presence there was a lawful use of the highway.

(6) In determining whether any liability for damage under section 4 of this Act is excluded by subsection (1) of this section the damage shall not be treated as due to the fault of the person suffering it by reason only that he could have prevented it by fencing; but a person is not liable under that section where it is proved that the straying of the livestock on to the land would not have occurred but for a breach by any other person, being a person having an interest in the land, of a duty to fence.

6.—(1) The following provisions apply to the interpretation of sections 2 to 5 of this Act. *Interpretation of certain expressions used in sections 2 to 5.*

(2) A dangerous species is a species—

(a) which is not commonly domesticated in the British Islands; and

(b) whose fully grown animals normally have such characteristics that they are likely, unless restrained, to cause severe damage or that any damage they may cause is likely to be severe.

(3) Subject to subsection (4) of this section, a person is a keeper of an animal if—

(a) he owns the animal or has it in his possession; or

(b) he is the head of a household of which a member under the age of sixteen owns the animal or has it in his possession;

and if at any time an animal ceases to be owned by or to be in the possession of a person, any person who immediately before that time was a keeper thereof by virtue of the preceding provisions of this subsection continues to be a keeper of the animal until another person becomes a keeper thereof by virtue of those provisions.

(4) Where an animal is taken into and kept in possession for the purpose of preventing it from causing damage or of restoring it to its owner, a person is not a keeper of it by virtue only of that possession.

(5) Where a person employed as a servant by a keeper of an animal incurs a risk incidental to his employment he shall not be treated as accepting it voluntarily.

Detention and sale of trespassing livestock

Detention and sale of trespassing livestock.

7.—(1) The right to seize and detain any animal by way of distress damage feasant is hereby abolished.

(2) Where any livestock strays on to any land and is not then under the control of any person the occupier of the land may detain it, subject to subsection (3) of this section, unless ordered to return it by a court.

(3) Where any livestock is detained in pursuance of this section the right to detain it ceases—

(a) at the end of a period of forty-eight hours, unless within that period notice of the detention has been given to the officer in charge of a police station and also, if the person detaining the livestock knows to whom it belongs, to that person; or

(b) when such amount is tendered to the person detaining the livestock as is sufficient to satisfy any claim he may have under section 4 of this Act in respect of the livestock; or

(c) if he has no such claim, when the livestock is claimed by a person entitled to its possession.

(4) Where livestock has been detained in pursuance of this section for a period of not less than fourteen days the person detaining it may sell it at a market or by public auction, unless proceedings are then pending for the return of the livestock or for any claim under section 4 of this Act in respect of it.

(5) Where any livestock is sold in the exercise of the right conferred by this section and the proceeds of the sale, less the costs thereof and any costs incurred in connection with it, exceed the amount of any claim under section 4 of this Act which the vendor had in respect of the livestock, the excess shall be recoverable from him by the person who would be entitled to the possession of the livestock but for the sale.

(6) A person detaining any livestock in pursuance of this section is liable for any damage caused to it by a failure to treat it with reasonable care and supply it with adequate food and water while it is so detained.

(7) References in this section to a claim under section 4 of this Act in respect of any livestock do not include any claim under that section for damage done by or expenses incurred in respect of the livestock before the straying in connection with which it is detained under this section.

Animals straying on to highway

8.—(1) So much of the rules of the common law relating to liability for negligence as excludes or restricts the duty which a person might owe to others to take such care as is reasonable to see that damage is not caused by animals straying on to a highway is hereby abolished.

<small>Duty to take care to prevent damage from animals straying on to the highway.</small>

(2) Where damage is caused by animals straying from unfenced land to a highway a person who placed them on the land shall not be regarded as having committed a breach of the duty to take care by reason only of placing them there if—

    (a) the land is common land, or is land situated in an area where fencing is not customary, or is a town or village green ; and

    (b) he had a right to place the animals on that land.

Protection of livestock against dogs

9.—(1) In any civil proceedings against a person (in this section referred to as the defendant) for killing or causing injury to a dog it shall be a defence to prove—

<small>Killing of or injury to dogs worrying livestock</small>

    (a) that the defendant acted for the protection of any livestock and was a person entitled to act for the protection of that livestock ; and

    (b) that within forty-eight hours of the killing or injury notice thereof was given by the defendant to the officer in charge of a police station.

(2) For the purposes of this section a person is entitled to act for the protection of any livestock if, and only if—

    (a) the livestock or the land on which it is belongs to him or to any person under whose express or implied authority he is acting ; and

    (b) the circumstances are not such that liability for killing or causing injury to the livestock would be excluded by section 5(4) of this Act.

(3) Subject to subsection (4) of this section, a person killing or causing injury to a dog shall be deemed for the purposes of this section to act for the protection of any livestock if, and only if, either—

    (a) the dog is worrying or is about to worry the livestock and there are no other reasonable means of ending or preventing the worrying ; or

    (b) the dog has been worrying livestock, has not left the vicinity and is not under the control of any person and there are no practicable means of ascertaining to whom it belongs.

(4) For the purposes of this section the condition stated in either of the paragraphs of the preceding subsection shall be

deemed to have been satisfied if the defendant believed that it was satisfied and had reasonable ground for that belief.

(5) For the purposes of this section—

(a) an animal belongs to any person if he owns it or has it in his possession; and

(b) land belongs to any person if he is the occupier thereof.

Supplemental

Application of certain enactments to liability under sections 2 to 4.
1945 c. 28.

10. For the purposes of the Fatal Accidents Acts 1846 to 1959, the Law Reform (Contributory Negligence) Act 1945 and the Limitation Acts 1939 to 1963 any damage for which a person is liable under sections 2 to 4 of this Act shall be treated as due to his fault.

General interpretation.

1965 c. 64.

11. In this Act—

"common land", and "town or village green" have the same meanings as in the Commons Registration Act 1965;

"damage" includes the death of, or injury to, any person (including any disease and any impairment of physical or mental condition);

"fault" has the same meaning as in the Law Reform (Contributory Negligence) Act 1945;

"fencing" includes the construction of any obstacle designed to prevent animals from straying;

"livestock" means cattle, horses, asses, mules, hinnies, sheep, pigs, goats and poultry, and also deer not in the wild state and, in sections 3 and 9, also, while in captivity, pheasants, partridges and grouse;

"poultry" means the domestic varieties of the following, that is to say, fowls, turkeys, geese, ducks, guinea-fowls, pigeons, peacocks and quails; and

"species" includes sub-species and variety.

Application to Crown.

1947 c. 44.

12.—(1) This Act binds the Crown, but nothing in this section shall authorise proceedings to be brought against Her Majesty in her private capacity.

(2) Section 38(3) of the Crown Proceedings Act 1947 (interpretation of references to Her Majesty in her private capacity) shall apply as if this section were contained in that Act.

Short title, repeal, commencement and extent.
1906 c. 32.

13.—(1) This Act may be cited as the Animals Act 1971.

(2) The following are hereby repealed, that is to say—

(a) in the Dogs Act 1906, subsections (1) to (3) of section 1; and (*b*) in section 1(1) of the Dogs (Amendment) Act 1928 the words " in both places where that word occurs ".

(3) This Act shall come into operation on 1st October 1971.

(4) This Act does not extend to Scotland or to Northern Ireland.

PRODUCED IN ENGLAND BY SWIFT PRINTERS (SALES) LTD
FOR BERNARD M THIMONT
Controller of Her Majesty's Stationery Office and Queen's Printer of Acts of Parliament

Appendix C:
The Writ of Summons

In the High Court of Justice
QUEEN'S BENCH DIVISION

1975.- T .-No. 3102

A.1
Ordinary Writ
(Unliquidated
Demand)

Oyez Publishing
Limited
Oyez House
237 Long Lane
London SE1 4PU
a subsidiary of
The Solicitors' Law
Stationery Society
Limited

F3367 12-9-74 BW17722

Between OLIVER TWIST

(an infant, by his father and next friend,

ARTHUR ALBERT TWIST)

Plaintiff

and

WEST MIDDLESEX SALVAGE COMPANY LIMITED

Defendants

Elizabeth the Second, by the Grace of God, of the United Kingdom of Great Britain and Northern Ireland and of Our other Realms and Territories Queen, Head of the Commonwealth, Defender of the Faith:
To WEST MIDDLESEX SALVAGE COMPANY LIMITED

whose registered office is at 201 Uxbridge Road, Southall in the area of Greater London
WE COMMAND YOU that within 14 days after the service of this Writ on you, inclusive of the day of service, you do cause an appearance to be entered for you in an action at the suit of

OLIVER TWIST

and take notice that in default of you so doing the Plaintiff may proceed therein, and judgment may be given in your absence.

Witness, Frederick Baron Elwyn-Jones

, Lord High Chancellor of Great Britain, the 26th day of July 1975.

Note. This Writ may not be served later than 12 calendar months beginning with the above date unless renewed by order of the Court.

DIRECTIONS FOR ENTERING APPEARANCE
The Defendant may enter an appearance in person or by a Solicitor either (1) by handing in the appropriate forms, duly completed, at the Central Office, Royal Courts of Justice, Strand, London, WC2A 2LL or (2) by sending them to that office by post. The appropriate forms may be obtained by sending a postal order for 14p with an addressed envelope, foolscap size, to the Clerk of Accounts Account Office Royal Courts of Justice, Strand, London, WC2A 2LL.

[over

Appendix D:
How to enter the legal profession

There are two branches of the legal profession. You will have to decide which one appeals to you, although it is always possible to change from one to the other later, if you fulfil certain requirements. The first approach is to become a Barrister; the other is to become a Solicitor.

Barristers have the conduct of trials in all Courts throughout the land. They have to be good at speaking, and in their use of words, and in preparing and presenting arguments. They also may specialise in some aspect of the law—such as taxation, family matters, crime. Barristers at present number about 4,000 (as against 40,000 Solicitors) and from their ranks are drawn the highest judges, as well as Circuit Judges, Stipendiary Magistrates and Chairmen of Tribunals. You have to have a good knowledge of the law and good health, because you will often have to do a lot of travelling and present a case in court with very little notice. It is also a risky business: no-one owes you a living and you have to impress Solicitors, who give you work, with your abilities and competence. Thus, in the early years of practice, at least, you cannot depend on the Bar to provide you with much in the way of income. However, becoming a Barrister may also lead to employed work with the legal departments of business, industry and government.

Solicitors, on the other hand, deal with the public. Barristers are not allowed to get work from the public directly, only through Solicitors. If you like the idea of working in an office and meeting people and helping them with their everyday problems, then probably the Solicitors' branch will appeal to you. It still means that you have to have a command of language and a good understanding of the law: for Solicitors can represent their clients in the lower courts, such as

Magistrates' Courts and County Courts. Some judges are now being appointed from the ranks of Solicitors. After you have passed your examinations, and undergone a period of apprenticeship, called 'serving articles', you may find fairly well-paid employment as an Assistant Solicitor, rising from there to become a partner in a firm of Solicitors, sharing in the risks and profits of the business. As in the case of Barristers, there are opportunities to enter employment with commerce, industry and government.

Qualifications

(a) The Bar

You have now to obtain a degree, preferably in law, from one of the universities or polytechnics, and the standard required is at least II (ii) honours. The subjects which you take at 'A' level depend very much on the university or polytechnic which you seek to enter, and you should read their prospectuses. After taking a degree, you will also have to attend the Inns of Court School of Law for one year and pass the Bar Examination. You may then be 'called to the Bar of England and Wales' by the Inn of your choice. There are four Inns: Lincoln's, Gray's, Middle Temple and Inner Temple. They are really colleges of Barristers and they offer comradeship and guidance, library and dining facilities. Each Inn will require you to eat three dinners each legal 'term' for eight terms, before Call to the Bar, which means being present in Hall and dining with other students and the Benchers (Judges and Senior Barristers) 24 times. After Call you are required to complete another four terms of dining. So you will want to join an Inn before you finish your degree. It is very much up to you which Inn you join: but you may have relatives or friends who are already members and you may wish to take their advice.

After Call, you will have to undertake two six-month periods of pupillage, which means unpaid tuition with a practising Barrister who will show you the ropes. During the second six months you may begin to do small cases in court yourself. Then comes the difficult (and highly competitive) task of getting a 'seat in chambers', which involves finding a set of chambers willing to take you on as one of a number of Barristers practising from an address in one of the four Inns of Court. It is not easy, finding a vacancy; but if you are persistent and present yourself well, no doubt in the end you will succeed!

Further information
Council of Legal Education,
4 Gray's Inn Place,
London, WC1

(b) Solicitors

There are a number of ways of entering the Solicitors' branch of the legal profession. Taking a degree in law at a university or polytechnic means that the period of training will be shorter. As a graduate in law, you will have to attend a year's course in preparation for the Final Examination and then serve two years under articles to a qualified Solicitor. This means that you get practical experience and training in a Solicitor's office, as an articled clerk, taking on responsibility for cases yourself, after a time.

But you could enroll as a student with The Law Society (the governing body for Solicitors) straight from school: you would have to have passes in five subjects in the General Certificate of Education, of which two must be at 'A' level, or in four subjects of which three must be at 'A' level. One pass at either 'A' or 'O' level must be in English, English Language or English Literature.

You must then study at a polytechnic for one year to take four subjects in the Solicitors First Examination. Then you take articles for five years. During the first two years of articles a further four subjects in the Solicitors First Examination must be prepared for and passed. Afterwards you attend a year's course for the Final Examination, and, having passed that,

Appendix D: How to enter the legal profession 129

return to serve the remainder of your period of articled clerkship.

If you take a degree in something other than law, you must first attend a year's course and pass an examination in the main legal subjects, known as Common Professional Examination. You will then normally attend a year's course for the Final Examination, and having passed that, serve two years under articles.

Further information
The Secretary,
Education & Training,
The Law Society,
113 Chancery Lane,
London, WC2

References

Page

1   *The Laws of Ecclesiastical Polity* (Routledge, 1888), Book One, p.129.

2   The case is *Harrison* v. *Duke of Rutland* (1893) 1 Q.B. 142.

3   The collective worship provision is s.25 of the Education Act, 1944.

4   *Monson* v. *Tussauds* (1894) 1 Q.B. 671.

4–5   *Commentaries*, Vol. I, Introduction, sect. 2.

5   St Matthew 22: 35–40.

6   *The Civil Law in its Natural Order*, Vol.I, Chap. 1, sect. viii.

7   *Ex facto jus oritur*—see Broom's *Legal Maxims*.

8–9   Plato, *The Republic*, Bk II, 368–9 (Jowett trans.).

10   Orwell's *Nineteen Eighty-Four*.

11   Lord Denning, *The Road to Justice* (Stevens, 1955), p.4.

11   *King Henry VI*, Part 2, Act IV, Sc.ii.

11   Archbishop Temple, quoted in *The Road to Justice*, *op. cit.*, p.1.

11   St Matthew 11, 28.

12   Plato, *The Laws*, 716.

14   The Chancellor's foot: John Selden (1584-1654).

16   Plato, *The Laws*, 864.

16–17   Plato, *Meno*, 97.

17   Plato, *Crito*, 51.

17   Atkin, James Richard, Baron, of Aberdovey (1867-1944).

References

17–18	*Donoghue* v. *Stevenson* (1932) A.C.562.
20	Plato, *The Laws*, 645.
20	*English Historical Documents*, Vol. II, pp. 480–1.
21	*Ibid.*, Vol. I, p. 373.
22	*Institutes of Hindu Law*, Chap. 8, 41–2 (Sir William Jones, Calcutta, 1794).
23–4	(1496) Y.B. 8 Ed. IV, 18 (Mich. pl. 30) as cited in *Law in the Making*, Sir C. K. Allen (Oxford, 7th Edn., 1964), p. 615.
25	Bracton, *On the Laws & Customs of England*, (Harvard, 1968), Vol. II, p. 33.
26	Sir Edward Coke (1552-1634): Co. Litt., 97b. Ulpian, Dig. 1.4.1.
27	Fortescue, *De Laudibus Legum Anglie* (Chrimes, Cambridge, 1942), Chap. ix, p. 25.
28	Lord Denning in *Ahmad* v. *I.L.E.A* (1978) 1 Q.B. 36.
29	De Lolme, as quoted in Dicey's *Law of the Constitution* (Macmillan, 1902), p. 40.
30	*Heydon's Case* (1584) 3 Co. Rep. 7a.
34	Edmund Burke, *Speech on Conciliation with America* (1775).
34	Blackstone, *Commentaries*, Intro. sect. 2.
34	Bentham, 'The Commonplace Book' (*Works*, Vol. x, 142).
36	*Bonham's Case* (1610), 8 Rep. 114, 118.
38	Ord. of Edgar: Stubbs, *Select Charters*, 71.
38	Hale, C. J., in *R.* v. *Taylor* (1676), 1 Vent. 293.
39	*A Man for all Seasons*, by Robert Bolt (Heinemann, 1961), p. 39.
40	Fortescue, *op. cit.*, p. 129.
41	See *The Order of the Coif*, Alexander Pulling (1884), for the history of serjeants.
45–7	*The Pickwick Papers*, Chap. 34.

48	Dr Johnson, as quoted by Lord Simon (1977) 1 A.E.R. 606.
50–1	Du Cann, *The Art of the Advocate* (Pelican, 1964), p. 41.
52	Erskine, as recorded in *The Road to Justice, op. cit.*, p. 56.
53–4	*Ibid.*, p. 58–9.
55	F. E. Smith—quoted in *Some Pillars of English Law*, Duhamel and Smith (Pitman, 1959), p. 113.
56	Erskine, as quoted in Denning, *ibid.*, p. 54.
60	Per Fortescue J. in *Reynolds* v. *Clarke* (1726) 1 Strange, 634.
60–1	*Scott* v. *Shepherd* (1773) 2 W. Blackstone 892.
61	*Donoghue* v. *Stevenson* (1932) A.C. 562.
62	*Robert Addie & Sons* v. *Dumbreck* (1929) A.C. 358.
62–3	*British Railways Board* v. *Herrington* (1972) 1 A.E.R. 749.
66	*Carlill* v. *Carbolic Smoke Ball Co.* (1893) 1 Q.B. 256.
66	*Slade's Case* (1602) 4 Co. Rep., 91a, 92b.
67–8	*Nash* v. *Inman* (1908) 2 K.B. 1.
68	*De Francesco* v. *Barnum* (1890) 45 Ch. D., 430.
69	Alderson, B. in *Hadley* v. *Baxendale* (1854) 9 Ex 341.
70	See e.g. *Krell* v. *Henry* (1903) 2 K.B. 740. One of the best and simplest of guides to the law of contract is the Concise College Text, *Contract*, by F. R. Davies (Sweet & Maxwell, 1970).
70	*Chandelor* v. *Lopus*, as quoted by Lord Denning, *The Discipline of Law* (Butterworths, 1979), p. 33.
71	Maine, *Ancient Law*, Chap. V.
74	More's *Utopia*, as quoted in *English Village Community and Enclosure Movements*, W. E. Tate (Gollancz, 1967), pp. 64–5.
74–5	Coke's comments on *Tyrringham's Case* (1584), 4 Co. Rep. 36B.

76	*Mayor of Bradford* v. *Pickles*, 64 L.J.Ch. 759.
77	Co. Litt., 1—1—Sect 1, 4a.
79	Churchill, Vol. 1, p. 137 (Cassell).
79	*Richard II*, Act II, Sc. 1.
79–80	*Commentaries*, Vol. II, chap. 1.
83	Viscount Sankey, L.C., in *Woolmington* v. *D.P.P.* (1935) A.C. 462.
83	'Nemo debet . . .' See Broom's *Legal Maxims*.
84	*Prohibitions del Roy*, 12 Rep.63.
84	Bracton (Harvard 1968), Vol. II, p. 33.
84–5	Lord Kenyon, C.J., in *Fowler* v. *Padget* (1789) 7 T.R. 514.
86–7	As translated by McKechnie, *Magna Carta* (Maclehose, 1905), p. 436.
86	*Commentaries*, Book IV, Chap. 27.
88	*Liversidge* v. *Anderson* (1942), A.C. 206.
88–90	See p. 132 *et seq.*, *Lord Atkin*, by G. Lewis (Butterworths, 1983).
91	*The Times*, 18 July 1983.

Index

Alfred, King, 21
Appeal, Court of, 45
Atkin, Lord, 17, 88–90

Barristers, 42, 51
Bentham, Jeremy, 34
Bill, in Parliament, 36
Bishop, 38
Blackstone, Sir W.
  on law of nature, 4
  on happiness, 34
  on property, 79–80
  on juries, 86–7
Bracton, 84
Burke, Edmund, 34

Christianity, basis of English law, 10, 38
Churchill, Sir W., 78–9
Coke, Chief Justice
  on reason, 26
  on acts of parliament, 36
  on enclosures, 74
  on land, 77
  on king and courts, 83
Common law, 20 *et seq.*
Conscience, 14
Contract, 3, 65 *et seq.*
Courts, 38 *et seq.*
Crime, 81 *et seq.*
Cross-examination, 54–5
Curtana, sword of mercy, 13
Customs, 7, 23, 40

Defamation, 4
Denning, Lord, 15
  on justice, 11
  on EEC law, 28
  on jury trial, 53
Dickens, Charles.
  Bleak House, 15
  Pickwick Papers, 45–7
Domat, Jean, 6

Earl (earldorman), 38
Education Act, 1944, 3
Equity, 14, 78
Erskine, Thomas, 52, 56
Estate in land, 77
European Economic Community, 28

Factories Acts, 31
Facts, law arises from, 25
Feudal system, 78
Fortescue, Chief Justice
  on political rule, 27
  on judges, 40
Freedom, 27, 34, 88, 91

Henry II, King, 20, 40
Hooker, Richard, 1
House of Lords, 45
Judges, 38 *et seq.*
  itinerant, 20
  use of reason, 24
  independent, 83
Juries, 45, 52–3, 85, 87–8
Justice, 8, 11 *et seq.*

King, under God and law, 25, 84

Index

Lawyers, 48 *et seq.*
Liberty, 33
Lord Chancellor, 14, 73

Magna Carta, 86
Manu, Laws of, 22
Mercy, 13
More, Sir Thomas, 38, 39, 74

Natural law, 7, 13
Negligence, law of, 18, 32, 61

Oath, of Judges, 38, 84
Opinion, of the best, 16, 19
Orwell, George, 10

Parliament, 29,
    Acts of, 30, 33, 35
    High Court of, 35
Peace, King's (or Queen's), 2, 43, 58, 82
Plato, on justice, 12
    on common law, 20
Prince of Wales, HRH, 91
Property, 73 *et seq.*

Queen
    mercy of, 13
    under God and law, 25, 84

HM Queen Elizabeth, 33
    in Parliament, 35
    assent by, 36
    and ownership of land, 76
Queen's Counsel 42

Reason, 8, 26, 29, 89
Roman Law, 26, 32

Serjeants-at-law, 41
Shakespeare, W., 79
Sheriff, 38
Socrates
    on justice, 8, 16
    on knowledge and opinion, 16
    on obedience, 17
Solicitors, 51
Status, 29
Statutes, 9, 29 *et seq.*

Tort, law of, 3, 57 *et seq.*
Trespass, 1, 23, 58
Tussauds, Madame, 4, 81
Tyranny, 10

United States, Supreme Court of, 36

William, King, 39, 78
Writ, 43